Some Sort of Bridge

In 1964 two recent Cambridge graduates, Adrian Bridgewater and Tony Watts, founded the Careers Research and Advisory Centre (CRAC). Their intention was to address a need that they had both experienced at first hand: the absence of reliable, independent and useful information and advice which might back up the significance of decisions about school exams, degree courses and careers. At the same time, the government and employers were becoming increasingly aware of the need to match prospective employees with the right occupations for the national good.

CRAC was a not-for-profit organisation that sought to 'build some sort of bridge' by using finance raised by donations and the profitable areas of its business to fund those that could not pay for themselves. Long before the phrase had become an accepted part of the business dialect, CRAC was a social enterprise.

Working often on a shoestring and relying on vision and foresight, CRAC's first ten years saw rapid expansion in both operations and influence. This book tracks that first decade, tracing the highs and lows and exploring the challenges and opportunities faced by this successful social enterprise as it grew.

The economic and social landscape has changed much in the intervening decades but the CRAC story continues to offer lessons, not only for those with an interest in the careers field but to anyone who wants to understand better how a social enterprise can develop and prosper.

Some Sort of Bridge

An early social enterprise creating
links between students and the world of work

DANIEL SMITH

The foundation and early years of
The Careers Research and Advisory Centre

Acknowledgements

It would not have been possible to write this book without the help of several former employees of CRAC and many others who were involved with its work. In particular, my thanks go to its founders, Adrian Bridgewater and Tony Watts.

I owe a special debt of gratitude to Brian MacArthur, Deborah Bevan, David Blandford, Klaus Boehm, John Brodie, Geoff Cooksey, Alan Jamieson, Mike Leonard, Mary Munro, Robin Mellors-Bourne and James Tomlinson.

Press cuttings and other images, for which we are particularly indebted to the *Daily Mail,* the *Economist, the Daily Telegraph,* the *Sunday Times,* the *Times Educational Supplement, New Society* and the *New Scientist* amongst many others, were digitalised by Paul Leahy from seriously damaged material; graphic design was by Lisa James.

I am most grateful to them all.

Daniel Smith

GRANTA EDITIONS

Published by Granta Editions
25-27 High Street, Chesterton, Cambridge CB4 1ND
Tel: 01223 352790 Email: booksales@bpccam.co.uk/book-sales.htm
ISBN 978-1-85757-102-8

Contents

CRAC

What is CRAC?

CRAC is the Careers Research and Advisory Centre. It exists solely to help parents teachers students and all others interested in careers. It is independent and gets its income from members' subscriptions. CRAC does not make a profit.

What services does CRAC offer?

CRAC aims to extend the knowledge of people who give careers advice, and offers three main services. First, it publishes a quarterly careers journal which provides a unique forum for discussion and for comment on current careers research; a practical link between schools universities and employers. Second, it answers members' individual inquiries, and for these problems it also has the help of consultants living in all parts of the country—the sort of problems which, while occurring all over the country, only occur in one school once in five years. Third, CRAC conducts research into career problems; employment patterns, salary comparisons, the transition from school to university or work, etc. In addition, CRAC sets up workable careers libraries for its members, and also runs careers conferences and courses.

Why is CRAC needed?

CRAC is able to provide objective and unbiased careers information for its members from its own investigations, but it can also publicise and popularise careers work which has already been done in schools, colleges, universities and the Youth Employment Service. CRAC seeks to complement existing services and to collect new problems for future research.

Membership of CRAC

An annual subscription of £10.10.0 entitles a school to the CRAC journal, and to make unlimited use of the CRAC Advisory Service. For £3.3.0 per annum a school receives the journal, but the use it can make of the Advisory Service is limited to one problem per year. The journal subscription rate is 45s. per year. *CRAC depends upon members' subscriptions to develop its work.* Full enrolment details and specimen copies of the journal can be obtained from:

The Careers Research and Advisory Centre
25, St Andrew's Street, Cambridge

This advertisement was presented to CRAC by
Hooker Craigmyle & Co. Ltd., 11, Old Burlington Street, London, W.1

INFORMATION SERVICE

C.R.A.C OFFERS HELP

The Careers Research and Advisory Centre are offering a new Intelligence Service, which will give sixth-formers, their parents and their advisers more information about the first degree courses offered at universities in the United Kingdom.

The service will be publishing course comparison bulletins. These will give details of the structure of the courses in a subject offered at the different universities. They will also analyse what the courses have in common, what are the entry requirements and, in more detail, the differences between them. Opportunities for specialization are listed, with an idea of the character of the course and a sample reading list for prospective candidates.

PARENTS' QUESTIONS

The other part of the service will answer questions sent to the centre of that the individual requirements of students can also be satisfied. The centre has an up-to-date reference library, and an advisory panel to deal with these kind of problems.

The intelligence service will become part of the C.R.A.C. services which schools receive on payment of an annual subscription of 10 guineas. Parents can pay five guineas and make use of selected services, including the intelligence service, or they can just pay 12s. 6d. to C.R.A.C. which is a non-profit-making body, for an answer to a specific question. Further details of the schemes are available from the centre at 25, St. Andrews Street, Cambridge.

First advertisement for CRAC services, *Times Educational Supplement,* August 1964; *TES* press cutting, 27 November 1964.

Introduction

For over 45 years the Careers Research and Advisory Centre (CRAC) has been a central player on the British careers scene. With such a long history, it can perhaps offer a few ideas to social enterpreneurs intent on innovation.

This short book focuses on the early years of CRAC's existence, from its inception in 1964 to its fundamental restructuring a decade or so later. Within this context, CRAC's start-up, development and restructuring can be described as an early example of social enterprise – a term which didn't even exist in those distant days!

Social enterprise takes many forms. Most often the social entrepreneur has identified a social need, a gap that might feasibily be filled by their enterprise. But to be a success the organisation must have a sustainable business structure so that it is able to provide the needed services consistently without running up losses. It may be that some of its services, though unlikely to make a profit, are intrinsically relevant and socially worthwhile. But since any organisation's guiding principle must be that its books balance and its operations are self-sustaining, it follows that each of its services must be individually costed. Where costs can't be met, donations or grants must be found to cover them so that the the enterprise can keep going. This particular social enterprise nearly took too long to learn this!.

In *Social Entrepreneurship: The Art of Mission-Based Venture Development*, Peter C Brinckerhoff describes the social entrepreneur:

'To me the core of social entrepreneurship is good stewardship. Good stewards don't rest on their laurels, they try new things, serve people in new ways, are lifelong learners, try to have their organisations be fonts of excellence ... They weigh the social and financial return of each of their investments.'

Chapter 1 of this book provides a short overview of the economic and social climate at the time of CRAC's genesis. *Chapter 2* looks at how CRAC's founders identified the national need for better careers advice and guidance. *Chapter 3* is concerned with the 'nuts and bolts' of setting up this particular social enterprise, whilst *Chapters 4* and *5* discuss how the organisation built and maintained momentum. *Chapter 6* describes how the careers sector had changed by the 1970s. *Chapter 7* documents CRAC's re-evaluation of its role and operations after its first ten years, and outlines the rationale behind its restructuring. *Chapters 8* and *9* look at how CRAC and its subsequent partner organisations evolved (and continue to evolve). The book ends with a chronology of CRAC's key early years and its final Report under Adrian Bridgewater's Directorship, in 1972.

Whilst CRAC's early years in many ways reflected specific characteristics of that historic period, its experiences still provide considerable food for thought today, not just for organisations in the careers field but for people considering starting up or expanding services as a social enterprise.

1
All Change for Britain

As 1964 dawned in Britain, the Beatles were topping the charts, Mods and Rockers were causing havoc on the beaches and Harold Macmillan's Conservative government was trying to find its feet amid the fall-out of the Profumo Affair. Whilst it is a truism that all countries are always to some extent in a state of flux, this was indeed a 'moment' in Britain's history.

At the core of this 'moment' was the realisation that the country needed to adapt to find itself a new role in the modern world. Any lingering suspicion that Britain was still a world power—a view that the optimistic could still cling to in the immediate aftermath of the Second World War—could no longer hold up against the evidence of a stagnant economy and a fast-dissipating empire, especially in the face of the Cold War: the swinging pendulum that dictated the global rhythm.

Britain's new position on the world stage had to be balanced against a growing domestic demand for greater social equality and mobility, rooted in the reforms of Clement Attlee's Labour administration of 1945–49. The post-war government had heralded in a period of high hope, fired by the euphoria of military victory and the return to peace. Taking its cue from the 1942 Beveridge Report on social welfare, Attlee's government oversaw one of the great periods of British social development, anchored around a programme of nationalisation and the establishment of the welfare state, with the National Health Service at its centre. The education system underwent a similarly radical overhaul, underpinned by a series of Education Acts between 1944 and 1947.

Post-War Education Reform

The '44 Act was chiefly the work of the Conservative Rab Butler, a minister in the wartime coalition, and in theory it promised a free and universal education system up to the age of 18. A government White Paper of 1943 had already asserted that education should be rooted in a child's 'capacity and promise' and not dictated by the circumstances of his or her parents. The pre-war set-up had seen schooling essentially in the hands of local authorities, churches or charitable foundations: it is estimated that something less than 15% of working-class children aged

13 remained in the education system in 1938. When Butler's Act came into effect in 1945, it raised the leaving age to 15 and introduced a tripartite system of schools. On the basis of examination at 11, children were destined either for the academic curriculum of the grammar school, the science- and technology-based technical school or the less academic secondary moderns that focused on developing practical skills and abilities.

Over the ensuing years, the dream of an open and fair education system for all remained a distant one. The new system, rather than breaking down social divisions, instead seemed to reinforce them. The tripartite system was in part influenced by Sir Cyril Norwood's 1943 report on examinations and curriculum in secondary schools. In it, three broad types of pupil were envisaged: first, those who *can grasp an argument or follow a piece of connected reasoning*, is *interested in causes* and can comprehend *the relatedness of related things, in development, in structure, in a coherent body of knowledge*; second, those who had interests and abilities best suited to the field of *applied science or applied art*; and third, those *interested in things as they are*. The danger was that this rather vague and subjective system merely reiterated outmoded class stereotypes: an upper class of 'leaders', a middle class of technocrats, and a large working class perceived as lacking both academic ability and creative imagination.

The hard economic realities of the post-war economy, overstretched and lacking investment, ensured that very few technical schools were ever built. They educated less than 3% of pupils and were significant chiefly as a theoretical talking point. Meanwhile, grammar schools remained overwhelmingly the preserve of the middle classes. The majority of other pupils were left to find a route into adulthood in the under-resourced and extremely variable secondary moderns. Secondary moderns *en masse* did little to promote ambition or to encourage social mobility among their student population, who were often left to contend with the self-fulfilling prophecy of being labelled 'failures' at 11. In 1963 less than 320 secondary-modern pupils went on to sit A-levels and not a single one found their way into a university. This was hardly the brave development of 'capacity and promise' that had been the avowed goal. As Law and Watts put it in their study *Schools, Careers and Community* (1977):

'There was a time, not very long ago, when it was possible to predict within quite tight limits the kind of roles a person would have by knowing three pieces of information – where, to whom and with what sex he or she was born.'

Economic Necessity

As the 1950s progressed, this situation was not only becoming unacceptable from a social and political point of view but was also becoming economically untenable. In Britain and throughout the developed world, there was a growing acknowledgement that education was not simply an end in itself but an important economic tool. A Government White Paper of 1956 reported Britain's competitor nations *'making an immense effort to train more scientific and technical manpower ... we are in danger of being left behind'*. Whilst this idea was nothing new—in 1946 the Barlow Report had urged universities to aim at doubling the number of science graduates—the sense of urgency was growing. Indeed, spurred on by the growing muscle of rival economies, and despite a general climate of austerity in the 1950s, education expenditure begin to increase.

In the twenty-five years leading up to the mid-1970s the percentage of GDP accounted for by education spending rose from 3% to over 6%. But throwing money at the problem was only a partial answer: little or no work had been done to attempt to quantify the qualified manpower needs of the national economy. One exception was the 1957 Willink Report which concluded, wrongly, that too many doctors were being produced.

A sea change in thinking was needed which would kill off the assumption that the public schools and select grammars would provide the 'captains of industry' whilst the secondary moderns would provide the numbers to work 'at the coalface'. If Britain's economy was to compete in the modern world, a much closer fit was needed between the requirements of industry and the talents and skills of individual pupils and students, regardless of their social background.

This sense that the educational structure should adapt to serve the needs of the wider economy was given further weight by the 1959 report of Geoffrey Crowther, chair of the Central Advisory Council for Education. He argued that education was a *'vital part of the nation's capital investment'*. He suggested a target of 20% of students going on to higher education, justifying the proposition thus:

'Can we conceive that it [the economy] will be adequately run by a generation of whom only one in twenty-five will have reached even a first degree? Is this not, in fact, a formula for national decline?'

Crowther also pushed for raising the school-leaving age to 16 by 1966–69, and suggested that sixth forms should not only prepare pupils for entry to university but also lay practical groundwork for those going straight into the working world.

The Robbins Report

The Robbins Report of 1963 fundamentally changed the pattern of higher education in the UK. Noting the resources of untapped educational ability, particularly among the working class (who made up a disproportionately small percentage of university applicants, even from the grammar schools), it recommended an immediate expansion of the university sector and proposed that Colleges of Advanced Technology should win university status.

At the beginning of the Second World War only 1% of 18-year-olds went on to a university education. By 1958/59 this had risen to 4.6% (as opposed to 20% in the USA). Post-Robbins, the numbers of full-time first-degree students increased from 92,000 in 1960/61 to 197,000 in 1967/68 and 217,000 in 1973/74. In such a rapidly expanding sector, Robbins pointed out the need for a closer relationship between universities and the labour market, and recommended that better information on higher education courses be available to young people and their parents – though the Ministry of Education offered no opportunity for publishers to tender for its provision.

The Association of Teachers in Technical Institutes responded to the Robbins Report in a pamphlet entitled *Is Robbins Enough?* The Association reaffirmed the need for tighter links between higher education institutions and industry:

'*Too many or too few entrants to any profession will produce serious problems for the community and the individual which would be avoided if some means of relating output to demand could be evolved.*'

Furthermore, they doubted '*whether sufficient consideration has been given to ensuring that the context of the University courses which prepare students for various occupations is in line with what their occupations require.*' The document's authors concluded that '*a formal relationship must be built up between each profession and the centre of higher education that supplies it.*'

The Technological Revolution

The question of how best to prepare school-leavers and graduates for the rest of their working lives did not merely occupy educationalists. The key role of education and training for the wider social good was put firmly on the national agenda at the Labour Party Conference of 1963. Harold Wilson (who would be Prime Minister by the end of the following year) set out his vision for an economy that embraced the benefits and absorbed the implications of technological and scientific development. He spoke of a nation that would be '*forged in the white heat of this revolution*' and that would be '*no place for restrictive practices or for outdated measures on either side of industry*'. But this revolution could not '*become a reality unless we are prepared to make far-reaching changes in economic and social attitudes which permeate our whole system of society*'. At least in part, this meant that for long-term economic wellbeing, it was key that the best people (from whatever social background) found their way into appropriate jobs.

Yet whilst there seemed a consensus that schools, universities and industry should work in closer co-operation, the question of *how* was much more vexed. The gulf between firms and schools was underscored in 1958 when the Carr Committee concluded that employers did not want schools to take any part in vocational instruction. Despite finding that there was a dearth of skilled workers, and too many employers failing to provide adequate employee training, the committee concluded that '*the responsibility for industrial training or apprenticeships should rest firmly with industry*'. The worlds of school and work, it seemed to suggest, were inherently separate and could not provide an overlap of knowledge and experience.

In 1963 the Newsom Report, which looked at the education of pupils aged 13 to 16 of average and less than average ability (which is to say, over 50% of the school population), pushed for more structured activities to prepare school leavers for what lay beyond the classroom walls. Reinforcing the Crowther Committee's recommendation for raising the school-leaving age to 16, it recommended that the school curriculum should be '*practical, realistic and vocational*'. The Brunton Report of the Scottish Education Board was the counterpart to Newsom, focusing on less-than-average pupils and also concluding that the curriculum needed to allow for a more practical strand, as well as vocational guidance from the age of 13.

Careers Work Pre-CRAC

The status of careers guidance in schools at this time is neatly encapsulated in Barry Hines' classic novel of 1968, *A Kestrel for a Knave*. In an exchange between the central character, Billy Casper, and his Employment Officer. there is an immediate sense of 'going through the motions', as the officer ushers Billy in for his interview: '*Well come in, lad, if you're coming. I haven't got all day.*' The troubled Billy has little idea of where his future lies and the options presented to him are limited to say the least ('*…an electrician, or a bricklayer or something like that*'). Finally the officer says:

'*Well if nothing I've mentioned already appeals to you, and if you can stand a hard day's graft, and you don't mind getting dirty, then there are good opportunities in mining....'*

Billy is adamant: '*I'm not goin' down t'pit.'* The officer is exasperated '*Well what do you want to do then? There doesn't seem to be a job in England to suit you.'* He sends Billy off with a pamphlet entitled *Leaving School*, which details sickness benefit and National Insurance, and has a detachable form to apply for his work card. The boy runs off into the day to train his kestrel, his future as uncertain and confused as when he stepped into the office. His capacities and his passions, symbolised in his kestrel, have received no attention.

The teaching profession itself was unimpressed by the idea of linking up employment and education too closely and fearful that schools would become mere factories churning out bodies for the industrial and commercial world. This type of attitude is to be found in a Ministry of Education pamphlet from 1947 which described the '*deadening routine of much industrial work*'. Many teachers who considered themselves progressives – a term that covered a multitude of meanings – saw education as being quite separate from wider economic goals.

The Start of CRAC

By 1964 it was generally accepted that there was a need for schools, universities, employers, students and their parents to understand each other and communicate more effectively. However, the structures that were in place to facilitate this communication were palpably not fit for purpose. So in March 1964 the Careers Research and Advisory Centre—commonly known as CRAC—came into being over a barber's shop in Cambridge to try and generate some of these much needed connections.

Anthony Sampson said later in his *The New Anatomy of Britain:*

'*The openings between schools and the outside world – whether universities, further education, or just jobs – are gradually being widened, examined and explained, and teachers and pupils are beginning to feel themselves part of a larger world. 'Vocational Guidance' is beginning to be a separate sub-profession. One pioneer organisation, called CRAC (the Careers Research and Advisory Centre) set up by an enterprising Old Etonian, Adrian Bridgewater, now provides courses, booklets and detailed information to explain to teachers the range of opportunities. As with so many other fields of reform (like housing or the health service) communications can be almost as important as legislation in breaking down the barriers; but the beating of new trails, the building of bridges and the dispelling of the fogs of ignorance will not be accomplished in one generation.'*

2
Seeing the Need

Adrian Bridgewater and Tony Watts first met when they were undergraduates at the University of Cambridge in the early 1960s. With three student friends, Bridgewater had started a *Picture Post* equivalent for students called *Image*, an accomplished and remarkably well-designed magazine. Alongside photo stories covering current issues, *Image* carried picture stories about young graduates at work, paid for by employers seeking graduate recruits. Bridgewater asked Watts to join *Image* to sell and then write these Employer Profiles

Bridgewater had graduated with a Law degree but no longer saw his future in his family's engineering business, in which he had spent three years before Cambridge. So, harbouring his new-found interest in publishing, he went to work for his magazine's printer in London, where he was conveniently located to seek out *Image* advertisers who had not paid their bills. One such defaulter was Cornmarket Press, a small publisher operating in offices above a Leeds clothmaker near Saville Row. Michael Heseltine, an aspiring Tory candidate later to become deputy prime minister under John Major, was one of Cornmarket's founder directors.

Cornmarket Days

Bridgewater insisted on waiting in Heseltine's office until the payment was secured. His stamina obviously impressed Heseltine, who rang the following day to offer him a job with his company. Cornmarket had been established in 1956 by Clive Labovitch and he was later joined by Heseltine to publish its *Directory of Opportunities for Graduates*, containing graduate recruitment entries for some 180 employers. Ewart Escritt, Secretary of the Appointments Board at Oxford, had long pressed for such a work and was on its editorial board. The book insisted on a standard format for each employer – regardless of its size – so that readers might easily compare the entries. Other titles quickly followed, including *Opportunities for School Leavers,* the tendentiously named *Directory of Opportunities for Qualified Men* and *The Graduate Employment Register.*

Bridgewater had an active role in developing the Cornmarket list and introduced the first UK Employment Register for Graduates. Meanwhile, Tony Watts, on his final long vacation from Cambridge, was being given a diet of threepenny pieces by Bridgewater to use in payphones to persuade personnel managers from assorted employers to buy Profiles in *Image*. About this time Labovitch had been approached with a half formulated idea for Cornmarket to publish a university guide. No detailed thought had been given to its content but the title was brilliant: *Which University?* The Robbins Report was then being drafted with its recommendations for dramatic university expansion. But many universities were producing nothing more than their official calendar which neither informed nor enticed prospective students. So the market was ripe for a comprehensive guidebook.

Labovitch saw its potential, bought the rights to the title *Which University?* for a small fee and started to work out how to produce the first edition of the book in 1963. Watts was brought in by Bridgewater to work on and plan the new publication. The following year, having completed his final year at Cambridge, Watts accepted a job with Cornmarket, which after a few months led to a freelance contract to edit a much enhanced second edition.

In their work for Cornmarket, Bridgewater and Watts were positioned at the centre of the debate about how to bridge the gulf between students, educational institutions and the world of work. They were regularly talking to people in commerce and industry, and in schools and in universities. A clear message was coming out. At all levels it was felt that students were receiving inadequate advice on the career opportunities open to them. It was particularly striking that university students (the nation's academic elite, no less) often said that they had received no advice on the right qualifications for a particular course or graduate career and appeared to lack a clear sense of why they were at university and what to expect after graduation.

Both Bridgewater and Watts had personally experienced the frustrating inadequacy of the careers advice at their respective schools and then at Cambridge. Both were convinced that this was a crucial issue. There was inadequate communication and even a sense of distrust between schools, universities, employers and students. At the school level, sixth formers going on to university were often admitted merely on the basis of their O-Levels (including Latin and Greek) and a teacher's recommendation. Meanwhile, Robbins had postulated that, subject to finding a course of study, two A-level passes should provide the right to enter higher education. The school honours board listing the pupils who had successfully entered a university was for many schools the 'High Altar' of their aspiration, as Robin Day described it in a 1965 Panorama BBC broadcast on access to universities post-Robbins. There was little encouragement to look beyond.

Careers Guidance Provision

For the school leaver not going to university, the most significant body involved in the transition from school to work was the Youth Employment Service (YES). From the early twentieth century there had been attempts to provide some form of careers guidance for school pupils. By 1909 a network of Juvenile Employment Offices was up and running, and the 1910 Education (Choice of Employment) Act provided for the Board of Education to play a role in helping children up to 17 choose employment. Further advances saw the foundation of the Association of Juvenile Employment and Welfare Officers in 1922 and then, in 1928, the Juvenile Employment Service under the remit of the Ministry of Labour. Nonetheless, the Service struggled, as there was a blurring of responsibility between the Ministry of Labour and local education authorities, as well as a suspicion in the popular conscience that the Service was little more than a junior version of the labour exchanges. Certainly, during the period of high unemployment in the 1930s, there was a strong emphasis on getting school-leavers into a job – any job – rather than providing a rounded advisory role.

The 1945 Ince Report triggered the evolution of the Juvenile Employment Service into the YES. Key to this development was a concerted effort to overcome the uncomfortable division of duties between central government and local authorities in a bid to provide 'universal vocational guidance'. However, in an address to the National Union of Teachers in 1949, Ince hinted at some of the contrary forces that remained within the service. Not the least of these was the government's belief that the YES had a crucial role to play in the restructuring of the devastated post-war economy. Working under the shadow of this weighty imperative, it was inevitable that there would be times when the interests of an individual might not wholly concur with the requirements of the wider economy. Ince said to the NUT:

'First of all, having regard to our economic position, they [the prospective employees] must be placed very largely in the priority industries and services of the country. Secondly, they must be placed in work suited to their qualifications, their interests and their aptitudes. These two considerations are not entirely compatible...'

By the early 1960s around two-thirds of local education authorities ran their own YES, whilst the other third opted for administration centrally by the Ministry of Labour. By 1962 there were almost 1,200 Youth Employment Officers (YEOs) at work throughout the country. According to the Central Youth Employment Executive (CYEE), the main functions of YES were to:

'...*provide vocational guidance for school leavers and other young people within these age limits, to help them find openings in employment, and to keep in touch with them during the early years of their working life.*'

By the early 1960s the Service was responsible for finding positions for around 40% of the younger (15+) school leavers.

As well as offering every pupil approaching school-leaving age an interview to discuss options and investigate openings, the CYEE published (via the HMSO) an array of materials including an extensive series of *Choice of Careers* booklets, a directory (the *Careers Guide*), various wallcharts and pamphlets on occupations for the less academically gifted, and a *Careers Bulletin* designed specifically for careers staff. Professor Alec Rodger of Birkbeck College had also developed his influential 'Seven Point Plan' for career decision-making.

Undeniably, the system had benefitted from the Ince reforms and was running more efficiently, yet still there were fundamental failings. The late 1950s and early 1960s had witnessed the rapid rise of counselling, with leaders including Ethel Venables, Peter Daws and Hans Hoxter in the UK, drawing inspiration from the work of people like Carl Rogers and Donald Super in the USA (Super's later association with CRAC is discussed in Chapter 7). Another expert in the field, Raymond Cattell, wrote in his 1965 work *The Scientific Analysis of Personality* that 4 hours was a reasonable estimate of the time required for an interviewer to make any serious inroads into a subject's personality. Yet the average length of a YEO interview was just 15–20 minutes, often conducted in surroundings that were hardly conducive to a helpful encounter. Few schools had careers rooms; careers libraries were a rarity.

Furthermore, in most cases the YES remained detached from the school careers teachers, with both sides often labouring in a climate of mutual distrust. As David Peck noted in *Careers Services: History, Policy and Practice in the United Kingdom*:

'*The quality of YEOs' work had improved steadily throughout the 1950s but professional relationships with teachers had been slow to develop.*'

This was a theme picked up in a 1965 enquiry into the future development of the YES, headed by Lady Albemarle who joined

CRAC's Panel of Advisers that year. The Albemarle Report pressed for a more cohesive relationship between YEOs, careers teachers, employers and parents. It envisaged a service offering a long-term programme of careers guidance, rather than a body that sought to place a school leaver into a first job almost regardless of the pupil's abilities and aspirations. The Report called for schools and the YES to work together so that careers education and guidance might be tailored to an individual's needs.

The Albemarle Report also highlighted a number of other ongoing problems inherent in the existing provision. For instance, it noted that *'only a very small proportion of careers teachers have received any systematic training'*. Elsewhere it made the point that:

'In the past the provision for careers information and guidance has been largely deferred to the pupil's last months at school. This is too late.'

The Report also called for increased research into the requirements of recruiters in specific industries as well as the broader study of employment trends. It was an agenda that had much in common with the programme being pursued by CRAC.

There were echoes of Albemarle in a 1967 report by John Evenden (the President of the Institute of Youth Employment Officers), which reviewed educational and employment policy in relation to careers work. Its recommendations included the mandatory provision of a service by all LEAs, access to external careers advisers for all pupils and students, and a re-titling of professional advisers as 'Careers Officers'.

By the late 1960s it was clear that the YES was flawed in its ability to do the job it had been created to do. Michael Carter summed it up neatly in his 1966 study, *Into Work*, when he wrote that:

'...children...come ill prepared to the world of work... the transition from school to work aggravates the situation, rather than ameliorating it.'

The Appointments Boards

From 1950 the public school sector had had its own careers organisation, the Public Schools Appointment Bureau (PSAB). Its origins lay back in the 1920s when Truman & Knightley, an educational agency, established a Careers Advisory Bureau which developed a devoted public schools arm in the 1930s. This subsequently became an independent entity and was restructured as the Public Schools Employment Bureau. However, in the post-War period when public-school leaver numbers expanded rapidly, the Bureau found itself severely overstretched.

The Headmasters' Conference undertook an extensive review of the service in the late 1940s. The Headmasters' Conference itself had been established in 1869, with membership confined to under 200 schools. Recognised as the mouthpiece of Britain's leading independent (and predominantly boys-only) schools, it had a significant influence on policy-making and its annual conferences were high profile affairs dealing with significant issues of the day. In relation to the Public Schools Employment Bureau, it recommended a full-scale overhaul, paving the way for the establishment of the PSAB in 1950.

The PSAB's remit was extensive. It aimed to provide pupils (more specifically, boys) with a range of information on careers, advisory interviews for school leavers and information on job opportunities throughout the country for careers masters. Furthermore, it sought to build better relations between member schools and the employment world at large and later set in place careers tests for A-level leavers. The organisation initially operated under a central council made up of headmasters and school governors, but soon regional offices were established offering work placement schemes, courses and information on industrial training programmes. Throughout the 1950s and into the 1960s, the PSAB was a powerful tool for public schools and for those of their students who were not going to university but were seeking industrial or other direct employment after school. Indeed, in the course of a visit to Winchester College to discuss CRAC, the Head Master remarked to Bridgewater:

'*Our own boys don't need these sorts of services. Almost all of them go on to university and the remaining few go into the Army or become accountants.*'

For undergraduates each university ran its own Appointments Board (UAB). By 1914 six universities (including Cambridge) had established Boards, with another nine following suit by the outbreak of the Second World War. However, by 1962 there were still only 50 full-time and five part-time appointments officers in higher education.

As their title implied, the UABs concentrated on job placement with little advice for students. Talks for students were usually vague and wishy-washy, covering 'personnel work' or 'opportunities in the retail trade'. Bridgewater and Watts had found their own student experiences of the Cambridge University Appointments Board to be unsatisfactory. A receptionist asked each visiting student: '*Which career do you have in mind?*' The officers of the Board specialised in the particular careers they knew – teaching, the Civil Service, women's careers, the Armed Services, industry etc. So a student's career might be decided before they ever got to meet their appointments officer (note the job title!). Looking back on the service in 1993, Watts wrote:

'The conventional wisdom in undergraduate circles was that they might be of some use if you knew what you wanted to do and simply wanted help in finding where you might do it.'

The Role of Employers

In the early 1960s the concept of the 'graduate recruitment scheme' was still in its infancy. The days of a graduate heading for the church, medicine, the law, education or the Civil Service (with a few engineers finding themselves in industry) were on the way out, but only just. Many employers thought graduates might bring brains but they might as likely bring too many brains: there was an enduring feeling that many employers benefitted more from taking on a hard-working school-leaver who could be moulded into the desired form. Until the late 1960s almost all accountants, for example, were recruited direct from school.

Nonetheless, a few employers saw the vast untapped potential of the graduate market and spearheaded the move toward developing more systematic approaches to finding and training the best people. At the forefront were companies such as Unilever, Procter & Gamble (then operating as Thomas Hedley & Co), Imperial Tobacco Company and the Civil Service. Unilever offered an unprecedented two-year graduate training scheme, whilst P&G's enthusiasm for placing graduates in senior front-line positions within a few months of joining earned them the reputation as 'Britain's first business school'.

Graduate recruitment in general was rather haphazard, with some three hundred employers going round the universities on a 'milk round', selecting from a graduate pool no larger than 10,000. Many employers, including the Civil Services, would send talent scouts around the universities, often conducting interviews or setting up visits before candidates had finished their finals. One or two employers, including the Army and GKN, sponsored undergraduates throughout their studies, and a few exceptional candidates were approached in their first year of studies. Very much a seller's market, it was not uncommon for graduates to take their pick from a half dozen job offers. Bridgewater for one, got fourteen offers, rejected them all and joined the printers of his student magazine.

Companies on the whole were woefully poor at providing information about themselves. Prospectuses, where they existed, were often no more than product marketing materials designed to persuade the reader of a company's infallible excellence. There was little serious attempt at providing objective information on the skills required by someone who was generally expected to spend their whole career working for them. As the Federation of British Industries commented in 1965, *'employers' literature... varies from excellent to lamentable'*.

A 1956 report from the Acton Society Trust (founded in 1948 as a charitable social science research institute by the Joseph Rowntree Social Service Trust) on the subject of 'Management Succession' highlighted several other longstanding problems with the system:

'Unable to recruit a sufficient number of able graduates, companies are turning to the later school leavers...Among reasons giving for preferring them to the graduates are that they are more adaptable and willing to learn and less conceited.'

The same report also illustrated the atmosphere of mistrust that could exist between recruit and company, particularly the complaint that some companies failed to monitor the progress of their recruits or to train them properly:

'As one graduate put it, a large company is rather like an elephant which sometimes takes you for a ride and sometimes sits on you and you are never certain which it is going to do.'

In 1964 Donald Stokes, then managing director of Leyland Motors, added indelicately to the debate:

'What distresses me is the number of boys with academic training who are completely useless.'

The belief of many firms that the introduction of graduate recruits caused more problems than it solved was a difficult obstacle to overcome. High among employers' concerns was the conviction that fast-tracked graduates unsettled the wider workforce. The 1956 Acton Report noted:

'The creation of an elite corps tended to spoil the trainees and to antagonise other employees... And finally, at the end of the training period, companies were apt to find themselves landed with too many 'nice' people not suited to any particular job.'

This rather bleak assessment of a precarious relationship was backed up by Anthony Sampson in his 1962 work, *The Anatomy of Britain*:

'The impact of unqualified, analytically-minded graduates on the provincial, home-grown world of industry has often been painful: in some firms after the war as many as 75 per cent of the graduate recruits had left after a few years.'

Nonetheless, the UABs had some allies in bridging this divide. A small number of employers were attempting to devise more successful ways of matching graduates to suitable openings. They sought to look beyond a candidate's class of degree or choice of institution, instead taking a broader view to find a rounded individual with the potential to fit neatly into a particular working environment. As Parry Rogers, who later became Chairman of CRAC, noted of his time as personnel director at IBM in the 1960s:

'...we were not concerned with degree discipline nor were we greatly interested in the class of degree achieved: what mattered was the right mix of personal qualities and brainpower.'

Attempts were made to bring some academic rigour to the selection process with test batteries and aptitude tests. Whilst much of this pioneering work was being carried out in the United States, a key player in Britain was the National Institute of Industrial Psychology (NIIP). NIIP had been set up in 1921 by Charles Myers, arguably the most important British psychologist of the first half of the twentieth century, and Henry Welch, who made his fortune as director of an East India merchant company. From early in its life, NIIP proudly sought to *'oil the wheels of industry'* by *'helping youth to the wise choice of a career'*. With a guiding principle that *'vocational guidance is the key to success and happiness in work,'* it carried out crucial work researching and developing recruitment best practice.

For schools, the Federation of British Industries tried to play their part, producing a somewhat clunky card index that attempted to provide pupils with information about the opportunities available to them. This index was to give CRAC one of its first major projects (see Chapter 4).

The Heyworth Report
The Heyworth Report on the UABs, released in 1964, gave the scene a radical shake-up, especially in light of the rapid expansion of the higher education sector heralded by the Robbins Report. Heyworth acknowledged that as businesses increasingly recognised the potential advantage in recruiting graduates, *'some sort of bridge was needed between the universities and businesses so that ignorance and suspicion on both sides could give way to something like mutual comprehension'*. The UABs, it was hoped, might be key to building that bridge. Indeed in their 1965 *Comment on the Heyworth Report*, the Federation of British Industries wrote:

'We regard the university appointments service as a most important link between universities and industry and as essential for the effective staffing of British industry.'

To this end, the Heyworth Report suggested the UABs should offer advisory interviews between appointments officers and students, provide information about careers, jobs and employers, and put into place systems to notify students of vacancies, to arrange interviews between students and employers and to deal with queries from employers. Additionally, the report recommended that UABs should organise visits into schools, in particular to talk about non-school curriculum degree course subjects, such as engineering, geology and metallurgy. They were urged to avoid simply being an employment exchange for graduates and were to focus on developing their advisory role. It was anticipated that to do this, there should be regular visits to employers, including those not yet part of the milk-round.

In order to bridge the divide between academe and the working world, the Boards were encouraged to include members representing both the university system and employment. Careers advisers would be expected to have the skills to deal with individuals on both sides of the canyon. The report was particularly prescient about the need for a cataloguing system able to cope with the imminent *'information explosion'*. This deluge of material would comprise universities' and employers' literature as well as materials on the subject of careers guidance itself. The careers libraries already in existence in UABs exhibited *'wide variations'* in quality, though the cause was certainly not a lost one.

The Ministry of Labour established a Manpower Research Unit (which made its first report in 1964) *'to study future manpower requirements and the future distribution of manpower between industries'*. For those in the careers field, it was hoped that increased knowledge of future recruitment needs would enable people to better plan a career path and help identify the most suitable areas of study and training. However, the Unit's links to government ensured that from the outset its work was hindered by high levels of bureaucracy and accusations of political bias. For instance, in 1968 the never less than acerbic Enoch Powell attacked it for the *'futile effort being expended by public servants'*. Nonetheless, with a growing understanding of its importance, manpower forecasting was an area with which CRAC would become intimately linked.

The Advisory Centre for Education

One organisation which offered a rather more hopeful glimpse of what could be achieved was the Advisory Centre for Education (ACE), established in Cambridge by Michael Young in 1960. Lord Young of Dartington, as he later became, was one of the great social innovators of his generation, forever seeking to stand up for the rights of those he regarded as disenfranchised or voiceless. In a long career his achievements ranged from authoring Labour's 1945 election manifesto to establishing the Consumers' Association and laying the foundations for the Open University.

In his classic 1958 book, *The Rise of the Meritocracy*—which sold half-a-million copies—he attacked the way in which the concept of meritocracy gave access to jobs on the basis of an applicant's merit (that is to say, their skill plus effort), which was giving rise to a *'new social class without room in it for others'*. In Young's own words:

'A social revolution has been accomplished by harnessing schools and universities to the task of sieving people according to education's narrow band of values.'

ACE was rooted in Young's belief that users of public services were no different from private-sector consumers. Taking lessons from the Consumers' Association, founded in 1957, ACE sought to provide parents with relevant information so that they might better engage with the school system and push for its improvement. The schools and local education authorities had notoriously failed to promote such engagement themselves, with the notion of parent governors and parent-teacher associations still something of an anathema.

In the first issue of ACE's journal, *Where?*, Young established the organisation's founding principles, which included:

'Parents of all income groups should have as much choice as possible, as well as the information needed to exercise it sensibly.'

This notion was based on the language of the 1944 Education Act that envisaged pupils receiving an education in accordance with the wishes of their parents. At the heart of ACE was a belief that the provision of relevant and accurate information would lead to increased dialogue between educational institutions and their various stakeholders, resulting in an improved and more socially equitable system.

Inevitably, Young's own background endowed ACE with a certain political weighting but the organisation itself was theoretically apolitical, favouring no particular policy or system. Indeed, he was quick to hand over day-to-day running of the organisation to Brian Jackson, whose background was in educational sociology. The goal was to empower parents to participate in the conversation themselves, and to this end ACE set about producing publications, running conferences and providing a postal question-and-answer service. In addition, ACE was happy to rattle cages, highlighting failings in the education system and striving to renegotiate the roles of schools, pupils and parents in the public mind.

Within a year, membership was running at 3,000 and had increased to

23,000 by the end of the decade, providing a consistent and important revenue stream, though it was something of a disappointment to some within ACE that the membership should in large part come from the professional classes rather than the working class, who most needed representation in the field.

It was perhaps inevitable that ACE offered CRAC plenty of lessons during its formative years.

The Students are Alive!

The Aims of Education, a collection of essays by the mathematician-teacher-philosopher Alfred North Whitehead published in 1929, was a further influence on Bridgewater and Watts. Dealing with education in its broadest sense, there is a guiding principle behind each of the papers that '*the students are alive, and the purpose of education is to stimulate and guide their self-development*'. Such an idea had obvious resonance within the terms of the CRAC project, as did Whitehead's assertion that '*education should be useful, whatever your aim in life*'. The need to engage the student and make the educational process a vital one was reasserted in his essay on 'Universities and Their Functions':

'*Knowledge does not keep any better than fish... somehow or other it must come to the students, as it were, just drawn out of the sea and with the freshness of its immediate importance.*'

Though not directly in Whitehead's terms of reference, this was perhaps no truer than for careers guidance, for so long and for so many a dreary and perfunctory component of their school or university life.

Bridgewater and Watts—youthfully exuberant, socially aware and full of ideas—found themselves working in a field on the cusp of great change, in terms of organisation and ideology. Although in their work with Cornmarket they had heard many comments and criticisms of the careers advisory services, they also came across examples of excellent practice which were evolving in isolation. They thought that these could be developed and applied countrywide. Crucially there was a dearth of accurate and up-to-date information. Advice on course or career choice would be useless without this. It was clear that there was room for an organisation that could provide lucid, accurate and independent careers and courses information along with training for teachers to develop careers advisory techniques in schools and beyond. Such a service could also provide a trustworthy bridge between the worlds of work and education. Here was the genesis of CRAC: providing, as Heyworth had put it, '*Some sort of bridge*'.

3
Laying Foundations

A new service—a centre which would collect and prepare both hard information and examples of best teaching practice, supplying these services to careers teachers and advisers—was an evident national need.

Bridgewater put a proposal to Labovitch and Heseltine outlining how Cornmarket might create such a centre, which would not only provide accurate and objective information to schools, colleges and universities, but would also identify, develop and disseminate materials developed from existing best practice in careers advisory work. It seemed certain that the pockets of excellence that Bridgewater and Watts had identified operating in isolation in schools and universities could provide the core of a much-needed service, along with newly collected and edited information and related training.

Although such a project seemingly offered significant benefits to an organisation already operating in the careers field, Cornmarket's directors, facing the day-to-day realities of an already complicated commercial business, could not agree to pursue it. Whilst the project expanded and evolved in the minds of Bridgewater and Watts, it failed to take off within Cornmarket.

But both believed in their idea and in principle were prepared to exchange their relatively secure financial positions in an established company for the uncertainty and risk of striking out on their own. Some of their ideas had been successfully applied in existing and new Cornmarket products but these fell far short of the potential of the service they envisaged. They were convinced about the need for their service, seeing it in clear socio-economic terms: young people were not getting the crucial information or advice with which to make decisions to advance their education and careers. It was even argued that the post-Robbins expansion of the universities would be at the mercy of the whims of misinformed applicants.

Neither Bridgewater nor Watts had money to invest in setting up an organisation and both had doubts about the ethics of making a profit out of students' and teachers' ignorance. However, despite these doubts and problems they decided to go ahead and Bridgewater told Heseltine they were leaving to pursue their plan. Heseltine tried to persuade

Bridgewater to stay on with Cornmarket but, having failed, unexpectedly offered Bridgewater a six-month notice period. This allowed him to complete his Cornmarket work whilst taking time to build up plans for the new project. The generous arrangement alleviated some of Bridgewater's financial worries and ensured his Cornmarket career ended amicably. An arrangement was also made for Watts to continue his work on *Which University?* on a freelance basis.

For Profit – or Not?

Over the next few months Bridgewater and Watts discussed the project with many potential customers including, in particular, the question of whether it should be run on a profit-making basis. It quickly became clear that to teachers the idea of a profit-making organisation with this agenda was questionable. From an employer's point of view, since the essence of the proposed initative was to build bridges and new relationships between educators and the world of work, the approach needed to be based on mutual trust. If the teaching profession was likely to feel uneasy with a profit-making organisation, then the consensus of opinion was that the structure had to be not-for-profit. It was to be set up as a social enterprise serving young people through improved services provided to both sides of the relationship—employers and educators—in the best interests of the student.

The more Bridgewater and Watts discussed the new service with potential users, the more their belief in its social need strengthened. As they began to analyse the risk, costs and benefits of setting up an enterprise to fulfill a social need, as against a straightforward company for profit, the appropriateness of the not-for-profit route seemed overwhelming. But their own personal sacrifices had to be considered: the removal of a secure career ladder, the lack of any salary during the setting-up phase, the direct costs of 'setting out their stall' and, above all, the impact of failure (not least on their own career prospects).

During the last month of his notice period at Cornmarket, Bridgewater received an unexpected promotion for a careers conference from ACE. He and Watts decided to attend and, with the permission of ACE, circulated a four-page leaflet outlining their proposed new service to canvass comment and support. Over 200 teachers attended the conference and a great deal of interest was generated. After the conference Bridgewater and Watts visited ACE's founder Michael Young to ensure that he didn't feel the new service was encroaching on ACE territory. Young confirmed that he considered ACE's role was to provide a forum for discussion but not to follow up their conferences with the implementation of specific outcomes. Indeed, Young saw it as a sign of their conference's success that somebody else was willing to take action. Both Michael Young and Brian Jackson, ACE's director, were very supportive and later suggested that ACE's part-time accountant, Howard Dickinson, who lived in Cambridge, might be available for CRAC too. The ACE course had been master-minded on a freelance basis by Klaus Boehm, who was a member of the University's Economics faculty and a Junior Research Officer at its Department of Applied Economics. Aware of CRAC's emergence, he became an adviser to the organisation in its early days before taking up a full-time position in 1966.

Nuts and Bolts

At Christmas 1963 Bridgewater's notice period ended. His most pressing problem was to decide on a centre of operations. By chance, an estate agent was advertising office space in Cambridge consisting of five rooms and a reception office over a barber's shop in St Andrews Street, opposite Emmanuel College. The rent was absurdly cheap at £100 a year (at that time the average price of a book was under £1 as against £15 today, but an equivalent rent today would be nearer £15,000 per annum). Still essentially a university city with a small population and not much industry, property prices and wages were much lower than in London or other large cities. The previous tenant had been a solicitor who had been forced to leave rather hastily having been struck off by the Law Society and the remaining part of the lease was available for immediate occupation. The University was the central focus of the city and St Andrews Street was ideally located for academics, student advisers and potential contributors to drop in. So the decision was easy.

Early in 1964 work began at 25 St Andrews Street and the first task was to finalise a name for the organisation. Tony Watts recalls the seminal conversation which took place in Bridgewater's kitchen. They discussed the Advisory Centre for Education's success in winning media attention, assisted by its catchy acronym, ACE. Seeing the importance of an easily recognisable and memorable name, they first chose an acronym and then filled in the words. CRAC stuck easily in the mind and sounded crisp and of the moment (lacking the narcotic connotations that would emerge in future decades). Working backwards from the acronym, the Careers Research and Advisory Centre seemed to describe the service they planned.

The next problem was to agree a clear statement of aims for the Memorandum and Articles of the company that would provide CRAC's legal framework. It was duly registered as a not-for-profit company,

which could be registered as an educational charity in due course. For this a governing council with at least seven members was needed; and crucially, if it was to gain charitable status, its stated aims had to be deemed charitable. Bridgewater therefore went back to a cross-section of supporters to create a representative Council and, at the same time, formalised a panel of Advisers. Members of both the Council and the Panel were carefully selected to reflect the precise fields within which the new organisation would be working. The Council of eight included the headmasters of a state grammar school and a public school, the secretaries of two university careers services, a university academic and a leading industrialist. Bridgewater was elected Chairman at the first meeting of the governing body and Watts was confirmed as a member. The much larger Panel of Advisers would support CRAC as its services were developed in the four fields of schools, further education colleges, universities and employers, with a fifth group concentrating on guidance techniques. People from each of these fields of operation were appointed over the first ten months.

Evolving the CRAC Brand

It was important for CRAC to evolve a range of services that would provide turnover, attract new subscribers and establish the organisation's identity as soon as possible. The desire to experiment and innovate needed to be tempered by CRAC's financial constraints and the immediate requirements of its 'market' (the subscribers and their end-users).

CRAC's core aims in its first year were defined as:

a) to help all careers advisers in schools, colleges, the universities and the Youth Employment Service, and

b) to provide an information link between education and employment.'

In April 1964 CRAC sent out a survey to all UK secondary schools and its findings formed the basis of the first plan for the organisation's future direction. A membership package was created that, for ten guineas per annum, provided four issues of the *Journal*, access to the Question Service and six or seven Information Sheets. Full membership was offered to Youth Employment Officers and Careers Advisers, to careers teachers in schools, to university appointments officers and to employers. Membership grew rapidly: by the end of 1964 it was approaching 1,000 subscribers. Although this provided cash flow, it barely covered costs.

It was soon clear that the Question Service presented particular problems because complicated questions were taking up to a day (sometimes longer) to research and answer. As quickly as a response had been sent, a sub-question could come back. The breadth of the service was indicated in an article in the *Library Association Record* of February 1967:

'Subscribers can ask for advice on all types of careers – questions ranging from the content of bee-keeping courses to openings available to graduates in oriental studies and psychology.'

Part-time staff were needed to maintain credibility and goodwill. Julia Allen, a full-time librarian in the Department of Archaeology and Anthropology at the University, offered to work in the evenings, not only answering questions but also to organise and classify the many books and pamphlets CRAC had begun to receive. Deborah Bevan, who had been employed in the Careers Advisory Service of the Middlesex Education Authority advising sixth-form girls on their choice of university, joined CRAC in the late spring of 1964. Having met Bridgewater at a conference, she recalled her impression that:

'CRAC was fizzing with new ideas. It was a very professional organisation from the beginning.'

Bevan's first task at CRAC was to get the Question Service under control, demand having spiralled as schools responded to having a resource to which they could turn at last. This she achieved principally by generating Information Bulletins from problems solved by the Question Service for wider distribution to members. Additionally, for the efficient operation of the Question Service and to meet CRAC's aim of making sense of the wealth of existing published information on careers, it was essential to get to grips with the CRAC Library. Although she had no formal librarianship training, Bevan laid out the basic guidelines for a careers library information classification scheme, based on the Dewey Decimal System. This ensured that one of CRAC's most valuable resources was manageable until the appointment of a full-time librarian could be made (see later in this chapter).

The Course Comparisons

CRAC published 29 Intelligence Bulletins in its first twelve months, spearheaded by the Watts-inspired series of *Course Comparisons*. These guides directly responded to a demand in the Robbins Report for an information unit to help young people (and their parents) who *'are choosing institutions and courses on the basis of inadequate knowledge'*. With a rapid expansion in the number of courses on offer, the Universities Central Council on Admissions (UCCA) was encouraging more students to consider the full range of possibilities. This meant that careers teachers (in those schools wise enough to have one), or more commonly subject teachers, needed to assimilate a wealth of new information, including information about unfamiliar non-school subjects. In response, Watts developed the series, with each of the *Course Comparisons* taking a single first degree subject (beginning with History, the subject Watts had himself studied) and providing a concise comparative analysis of the structure, content and emphasis of the degree programmes at all relevant institutions.

It was an idea of elegant simplicity and met a need that was not being met elsewhere. 39 titles were produced by 1966, covering Accountancy to Zoology via Chemical Engineering and Italian. The *Course Comparisons* (later renamed *Degree Course Guides)* were well received by sixth forms throughout the country, as were other Intelligence Bulletins on subjects including, for instance: *Progress in the Implementation of the Robbins Report; Mutual Recognition of English and Scottish Qualifications for University Admission*; *Technical College Courses in Computing Subjects;* and *Entrance Requirements of Professional Bodies.*

Following the publication of the first *Course Comparisons*, Bridgewater visited Marlborough College where the Master, John Dancy, urged him to make a charge for them over and above the Schools' Subscription '*because they are so excellent that schools are realising they can't manage without them*'.

But the Question Service continued to be a victim of its own success. In the course of 1965–66 it received over 1,400 enquiries. In the end subscribers were restricted to a single question per year, with a £1 fee per subsequent question. New Information Bulletins continued to be produced to cover the most popular questions. This put pressure on the budget for the Information Bulletins promised to full members. Gradually it became realistic to classify questions into topics so that further enquiries could be pre-empted by Intelligence Bulletins.

Early sources of help were Mary Munro and Julia Allen, both of whom worked for CRAC for a little over a year but went on to maintain a strong relationship. Mary Munro subsequently worked with the Careers Service at the Cambridgeshire College of Arts and Technology (now Anglia Ruskin University), where she established its careers centre. She would later write several key CRAC books including *Your Choice of A-Levels*. Remembering those early days with CRAC, she recalled the experience as '*extremely useful*' and described how CRAC '*showed the way that things could be done so that there was much better careers information in a very short time*'.

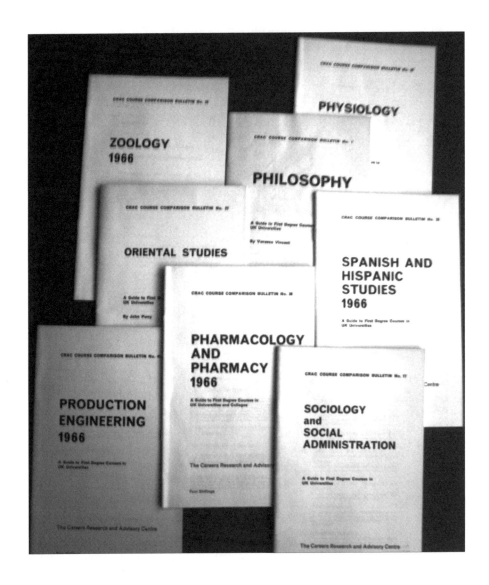

Some of the 1966/67 set of 46 *Course Comparison Guides* published and updated biennially by CRAC.

4
Evolving the Services

With the core elements now firmly in place, CRAC set about developing new services in response to need and opportunity. With finance at a premium, it was essential that innovation and experimentation were balanced against good governance. Thorough research ensured that CRAC's projects reached their market fully-formed and instantly useful.

CRAC's *Journal* and First National Conference

The first edition of CRAC's *Journal* was published in the early summer of 1964 and played a vital role as its public face in its early years, not only engaging with its paid-up membership but also prompting wider debate on nationally important issues. Edited by Watts, the *Journal* was structured around a number of regular sections. These included 'Forum', where problems or new ideas were discussed; 'Progress', for news and comment on developments in the careers field; and 'Perspective', for more general news. Lead articles often stemmed from CRAC's own work or research projects in universities, or were contributed by specialist writers. From the outset the *Journal* carried weighty and timely articles and in-depth analysis. And, as was to be expected given Bridgewater's publishing background, it was elegantly produced, with graphic design rules laid down by Phil Steadman, a Cambridge contemporary.

Of all the items in the first edition, it was an article by Colin Leicester on 'Economic Growth and the School Leaver' that had the widest immediate impact. Leicester was, like Klaus Boehm, a Junior Research Officer at Cambridge's Department of Applied Economics, which was studying '*the imbalance between the skills possessed by the labour force at any one point of time and the mix of skills required by the economy*'. He was a member of a team led by Richard Stone, the Nobel prize-winning economist, which was modelling the British Economy, with Leicester handling labour market matters. Boehm encouraged him to contribute an article for the *Journal*, which Watts was on the point of sending to press.

Criticising the manpower-predicting techniques then employed by the Committee on Scientific Manpower and the Ministry of Labour's

Men for Growth

TAKING the assumption that the economy will manage to sustain a 4 per cent per annum rate of growth between now and 1970 as his starting point Mr Colin Leicester of the Department of Applied Economics at Cambridge has used the Cambridge econometric model to predict how many scientific and technically qualified men industry would be likely to employ by the end of the decade. His answer is that it is likely to be two and a half times as many as companies employ now. His figures, published in the Journal of the Careers Research and Advisory Centre, are intended to show careers masters the kinds of jobs likely to be going-begging. They are not as wildly out of line with the government's own predictions as one might have expected. Mr Leicester set about his calculations in the first place because he mistrusted the basis used by Mr Hogg's Committee on Scientific Manpower to make its predictions. The committee merely asks companies how many scientists, and of what kinds, each thinks it will be employing three years from now. The answers always come out wrong, and the committee has now its own empirical way of weighting the evidence; the increase of 25 per cent in the demand for scientists between 1962 and 1965 that it forecast last year was its own conclusion, not simply what the raw answers from business suggested.

If demand were to go on increasing at this rate, with nearly half the qualified men being employed in manufacturing industry (the only field covered by Mr Leicester), technical and scientific employment by 1970 would be within shouting distance of Mr Leicester's estimate. If allowance is made for the tendency for the employment of scientists in industry to increase at a rather faster rate than in other fields, the two sets of calculations match up surprisingly well, considering that both of them are based on some pretty sweeping assumptions. The chart shows Mr Leicester's top eight qualifications, showing the extra numbers needed, on his calculations, by 1970.

Since he was writing for careers masters, he hardly needed to point out something they probably know perfectly well—that mechanical engineers may be in top demand, but boys are just not taking up mechanical engineering. There are two scientific jobs among the top five, and " outside the top five (who amount to more than three quarters of the total) everybody is relatively small beer." The switch, in terms of employment opportunities from scientists and towards engineers is something that has been stressed by every report on scientific manpower published here and in Europe during the past year. Careers masters can draw their own conclusions.

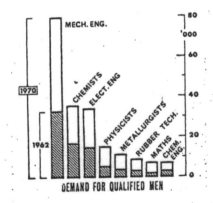

DEMAND FOR QUALIFIED MEN

Manpower Research Unit, Leicester sketched out his Department's 'Cambridge Growth Project Model', which related manpower demand to a composite model of the whole economy. The data could then be used to advise students about to embark on a degree about which subjects were likely to be most valued by employers in the years to come. For instance, the table opposite illustrates how the Cambridge Model projected that the manufacturing sector would be most in need of mechanical engineers by 1970, whilst demand for, say, geologists would be relatively insignificant.

In his conclusion, Leicester explained how this data might, and should, be used in terms of careers guidance:

'Firstly, there really must be sufficient places for them at the universities and other institutions of further education. Secondly, boys and girls must be encouraged, at the right moment before they leave school, to aim for the avenue with most opportunities. Thirdly, since no amount of talking can turn arts students into physicists at the last moment, the syllabus from which the school-leaver has drawn his education must also, so to speak, be pointing in the right direction.'

Whilst aimed at those working in the careers field, Leicester's article included themes of interest to statisticians, economists and politicians. Its impact on the national press was massive. 'Economic Growth and the School Leaver' was reproduced in the *Daily Telegraph* in full – giving rise to quite heated correspondence – and was encapsulated in almost every national paper and many trade magazines. It was a highly effective exercise in illustrating how careers guidance could fit into the wider national picture.

Other articles in the first edition highlight how CRAC engaged with key issues of the day. 'Graduate Careers and the Sixth Former', by A.J. Caston of the University of London Appointments Board, connected the problem of forecasting future demand for graduates with historical career paths of graduates by discipline. 'Stagnation in Vocational Guidance?' by Alec Rodger, the first Professor of Occupational Psychology at Birkbeck College, addressed the need to engage young people so that they might be better informed when making career decisions. Elsewhere, the 'Forum' section focused on the problematic relationship between industry and the careers adviser.

Its first *Journal* put CRAC on to the national map and its publication roughly coincided with CRAC's first National Conference, on the theme of 'Higher Education and Careers'. Held at King's College, Cambridge, from 26 to 28 July 1964 and planned jointly with ACE, it was addressed, amongst others, by John Fulton (Vice-Chancellor of Sussex University and later Sir John Fulton), Peter Venables (Principal of the Birmingham College of Advanced Technology and later Sir Peter Venables) and Colin Leicester. It was attended by over 130 teachers and a number of YES officers, university representatives and employers. Its aim was to discuss strategies for advising school pupils on higher education courses and careers choices. The conference brought together representatives from each of the key groups—schools, universities and employers.

The conference at King's marked the start of several long and fruitful relationships with future CRAC writers and conference speakers. In particular, Venables, who became Chairman of the Open University in 1969, would go on to play a significant role in the fundamental reordering of CRAC's structure (see Chapter 7), during the time when Bridgewater was serving on the Governing Body of the Open University under Venables's chairmanship.

Developing a Media Presence

The impact of the coverage generated by the *Journal* and the Conference caused a major surge in membership numbers, providing evidence of the power of press attention. Its media presence was important to CRAC not least because it was in the business of generating discussion. As early as December 1964 the journal *Personnel Management* had acknowledged CRAC's position as '*a means of communication rather than as a pressure group*'. The media had recognised CRAC's high academic standards which helped to establish it as a respected voice in the field.

However, spreading the word was a major challenge and initially CRAC had met with considerable media apathy. Roy Nash, then educational correspondent of the *Daily Mail*, told Bridgewater that education stories '*never sold a copy*'. But CRAC was quick to build up strong media connections, supported by a range of journalists who appreciated the CRAC project. Among the first of these were Virginia Makins, the education correspondent for the *Observer*, and Brian MacArthur at the *Times*.

Partly because of the Robbins Report all the major newspapers were employing education correspondents and they were beginning to be far more active. MacArthur, for example, campaigned for universities to do more to ensure that schools and students had reliable and balanced information. MacArthur recalled:

'Previously, 'careers' was done by some hapless teacher who had been corralled in to the role with no training and sent off to the school library to read a few university prospectuses. That's what it was. Most

teachers would know about their own university and a bit of gossip about others but they were not very well informed at all.

CRAC was a very fizzy, ambitious project and gave people a way of finding out things that had been very difficult to find before. Their materials were much better than anything that had been on offer beforehand. You had an outfit that campaigned for change and progress and transformed the situation.'

The wider media uptake of articles in the *Journal* became an important way of getting attention. Leicester's contribution was followed in the second (Autumn 1964) edition by a related article by J.K. Hudson, deputy appointments officer for Newcastle and Durham, on 'Employment Prospects for Arts Graduates in the Post-Robbins Era'. It reported on the mass of arts graduates predicted for 1981 (their number totalling more than the total number of graduates in all disciplines in 1964) and the problems they would face in securing employment. Because the universities were preparing to swell their numbers in light of the Robbins report, Hudson's essay gained significant coverage in the national press. 'The Needs of Industry' in the same edition, by Gareth Jones of Esso's recruitment and manpower division, drew still more media attention with its radical proposal of a tax-free bounty for first-class engineering and science graduates. Though the idea was a relatively small element in a longer review of ways to encourage an increase in the number of students taking up science at degree level, it was a strong and successful 'headline grabber' and tapped into a growing concern about a shortage of high-class scientists.

CRAC's in-house staff made their own efforts to bolster its media presence, often through correspondence with newspapers and periodicals. Letters of correction and comment were sent to a disparate range of publications, encompassing specialist titles such as the *Chartered Mechanical Engineer, Education* and others with more general readerships, including the *Times Educational Supplement* and the *Sunday Times*. Opening up debate was a constant theme, as reflected in a letter Watts wrote in 1964 to *New Society* (a left-of-centre socio-political magazine), criticising a report on university selection criteria. In it, he suggested that measures of academic and social standing then being employed were '*so subjective, so irrational and (often) so out of date as to be dangerous*'.

CRAC began to establish formal relations with most national newspapers and as early as April 1965, notwithstanding the earlier comment of Roy Nash, CRAC contributed a feature article, 'Careers

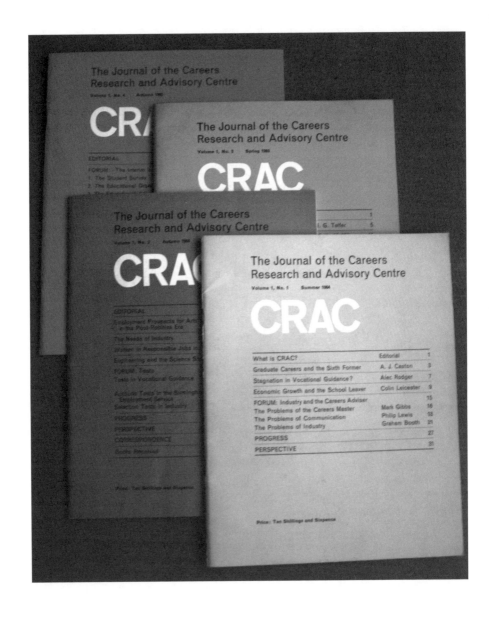

The first four issues of CRAC's *Journal*, each of which generated considerable press coverage.

for the Young… and Not So Young', for the *Daily Mail*. Others would follow, including a weekly presence in the *Financial Times* from 1967 (see Chapter 5).

The Economic Strain

Despite its booming Question Service, a strong demand for information, a very well-received *Journal* and a first Conference, CRAC's finances were hanging on a thread by the end of 1964. Bridgewater was taking no salary or expenses and Watts was dependent upon his freelance contract with Cornmarket to edit *Which University?* and a small fee (paid to CRAC) for editing *Outlook: A Careers Symposium* for MacDonald Publishers. *Outlook* was the idea of Robin Guthrie, the son of the then master of Downing College and an early supporter of CRAC who later headed up the Charities Commission. *Outlook* brought together young graduates from a range of professions and industries to give autobiographical insights into the realities of their respective working environments for the benefit of those a few years behind them. An updated second edition, co-edited by Guthrie and Watts in collaboration with CRAC, appeared in 1965. It did not earn CRAC a fortune. Bridgewater remembers a furtive visit by his bank manager one Saturday morning whom he spied circling his house, presumably assessing its value should he need to call in the Bank's loan!

Two major projects were occupying the management team full-time. The first was to nurture and exploit the growing interest in CRAC from the Federation of British Industries (FBI). Its Education Committee had particularly noted the Conference and the first *Journal* and had approached CRAC to enquire whether it could help develop and improve its Index Card Scheme for schools launched some years earlier. Its Head of Education, Jimmy Moore-Coulson, a former Director of Army Education, had attended CRAC's Conference and Bridgewater was commissioned to devise a new approach which could go before his Education Committee of teachers and employers. Apart from the representative from Allied Electrical Industries Ltd, a Mr Marshall, the committee fully endorsed the CRAC proposition to introduce a formal structure for the Scheme, making training information more easily comparable from employer to employer. Over 4,500 sets of the Card Scheme would be revised and reissued each year for a standard fee of about £25 (with 200 participants paying a total approaching £100,000 at today's prices). This contract, which was agreed in the Winter of 1964, greatly strengthened CRAC's finances.

The Appeal Fund

The second urgent project was to launch an appeal for funds in general support of CRAC's aims. Because of continuing favourable press coverage, there was now a belief among trusts and other potential sources of grants that CRAC was here to stay. The Society of Drapers came in first with funding of £500 per year for seven years; other trusts followed. Bridgewater engaged the services of the fundraising consultancy Hooker Craigmyle and was assigned Air Commodore Amlott, whose expertise in securing further grants soon justified his fees. His presence alone was enough to persuade CRAC's printer that its bills would be paid!

Amlott helped CRAC to produce an appeal brochure as the focal point of a high-profile campaign. The appeal's aim was to support developmental expenditure in three main areas:

1. *The Library Research and Information Services*
2. *Regional organisation*
3. *Office reorganisation.*

CRAC's cause received a significant boost on 5 February 1965 when the Conservative Member of Parliament for Perry Barr in Birmingham, Wynham Davies, introduced a House of Commons debate on the future of careers guidance in Britain. He argued that:

'*As the speed of progress in the cybernetic revolution accelerates, so the young employee of the future may need to change his type of occupation or work several times. A recent survey suggests that this might be as many as four times on his working life. A new conception, therefore, of continuous vocational guidance is required. Are we ready for this? Are we ready for all the implications?*'

He went on to suggest that in broad terms, the answer was 'no'. He mentioned CRAC, though, as an example of the kind of organisation that the sector needed:

'*I never fail to wonder at the sense of dedication and spirit of public service that inspires so many of this nation of ours… Amongst those active in the field of vocational guidance whom I have met over the past few days and weeks, I have met… an Old Etonian who, forsaking a safe job with a family firm, risked his own resources to provide a service in this field… Since there is even a lack of suitable basic information available, the new non-profit-making body called the Careers Research and Advisory Centre has been opened at Cambridge. It has been created to meet the need and has already 500 subscribing members. Since Hon. Members opposite often believe the Etonian to be the recipient of all the advantages of a good educational life, I have it on good authority that some Etonians feel that their career advising is as inadequate as that in many other schools.'*

Bridgewater and Watts were in the public gallery for the debate and recalled looking down into the chamber to see many members holding a copy of CRAC's appeal brochure. Buoyed by the attention generated from the parliamentary debate and the public relations opportunities it offered, the appeal forged on. *'I thought Christmas had come!'* Bridgewater commented many years later. Within two years of its creation, CRAC found itself on a reasonably even financial keel. It had learned the first lesson of social enterprise - no amount of idealism will win through if there are not firm economic foundations.

Picking Up Speed

Funds available in 1964 and 1965 were ploughed into an ambitious programme of courses and publications, with CRAC's management aware of the vital need to keep relevant services coming. In its first year it ran eight study courses that were attended by over a thousand employers, teachers and careers advisers. The post-Robbins revolution was a theme underlying several of these events, with CRAC aiming to provide a better understanding of the new opportunities available in higher education and their relation to the needs of employers. Thus, there were courses on 'The Role of the Technological Universities', 'Courses and Careers for the Arts Sixth Former' and 'The First Employment of University Graduates'. For pupils choosing not to carry on their formal education, ideas for career paths were presented in 'The First Jobs of School Leavers'.

Additionally, there were six conferences for sixth-form students (organised in collaboration with the Industrial Welfare Society) on 'The Challenge of Industry'. These looked at generalised problems faced by industrial managers, irrespective of their particular industry or company, and aimed to provide pupils with a greater sense of the realities of the working world. Run principally through discussion sessions led by managers young enough still to have something in common with their audience, they were held at Hitchin and Letchworth Grammar Schools, St Paul's School, Charterhouse and Winchester College. The concept of providing insights into the working world for those about to enter it would turn out to be among the most successful of all CRAC's innovations over the years to come.

The Robbins Report had recommended the establishment of graduate Business Schools in the UK (the first being established in London and Manchester). In 1965 J.C. Dancy, the Master of Marlborough College, took the radical step of introducing Business Studies into his school's curriculum, prompting much debate and strongly influencing the decision of the Confederation of British Industry (CBI), the successor body to the FBI formed in 1965, to support promote and develop the CRAC's Business Studies programme. Dancy's address in December 1965 at a CRAC conference on 'Business Studies Courses for the Sixth-Form Leaver' was a well-attended and widely-reported event, emphasising CRAC's ability to identify and respond to questions of pressing importance.

This skill was evident in the next *Journal* too. In June 1965, I.G. Telfer, careers master at Radley College, was the author of a survey into professional exam failure rates, which revealed an average 50% failure rate among candidates taking exams in eleven professions. Uncovering a pass rate that had not improved since the 1950s, it exposed an area of concern not only for the unqualified members of these professions who had little guarantee of exam success, but also for their employers who were sacrificing money, time and effort to put recruits through the process. The story was widely picked up by the press including the *Times*, the *Sun* and the *Observer*.

In November the *Journal* published the results of Watts's groundbreaking survey 'The Interim between School and University', which collated statistical and anecdotal information from almost 700 students at the universities of Cambridge and Nottingham who had experienced a period of time away from education after their sixth-form studies. It was followed up with a practical guide entitled *Students in Transition.* The interest of the wider media was once again pricked, with coverage in publications as disparate as the *Times Educational Supplement*, the *Lancet*, *Education*, the *Observer*, the *Guardian* and the *New Statesman*. No thorough examination of this 'gap year' had ever been undertaken before in the UK: it soon became an acknowledged element of many students' experience.

The Importance of Networking

While maintaining its policy of complete political independence, from its earliest days CRAC was alive to the need for (and indeed advantages in) nurturing working relationships with other bodies active in the field. It was, for instance, in regular communication with the Department of Education and Science, and was consulted in the drafting of the 1964 Industrial Training Act. CRAC also maintained good relations with local education authorities and with the Central Youth Employment Executive with a view to the overall development of its services. Other organisations with which there was regular contact and exchange of ideas included the Public Schools Appointments Bureau, the Headmasters' Conference, the Incorporated Association of Head Masters, the British Association for Commercial and Industrial Education, the British Institute of Management, the Industrial Welfare Society and the Institute of Personnel Management. CRAC's excellence at creating new links and connections was reflected in its working conference for 'Executives Responsible for Personnel, Manpower Planning and Recruitment', held at Magdalene College, Cambridge, in July 1966, which attracted representatives from seventy major UK employers.

In October 1964, the Schools Council for the Curriculum and Examinations came into being, with responsibility for work previously undertaken by the Secondary Schools Examination Council and the Curriculum Study Group. The Council incorporated representation from a number of educational bodies, most notably teachers' organisations, taking issues of curriculum development into the non-governmental sphere and allowing – it was hoped – a disparate range of stakeholders to exert influence on educational decision-making. Its establishment provided a vital access point for CRAC in its desire to develop careers education as a curriculum subject in all UK schools. The relationship between the Schools Council and CRAC grew over the years so that by the end of the decade and into the 1970s the two organisations worked closely on the conceptualisation and delivery of innovative school materials for careers teaching (see Chapter 6).

Library Innovation
The CRAC Appeal had generated around £30,000 by the Summer of 1966, predominantly from institutional donors. Although this fell short of the target of £90,000, it enabled CRAC to begin considering expansion, including development of the Library. In July 1965 CRAC had made a crucial appointment when James Tomlinson came in as Librarian on a salary of around £1,500 per annum found for CRAC by MSL, a firm of headhunters set up by Magdalene College graduate Harry Roff. Tomlinson, a graduate of Liverpool University, had taken his postgraduate diploma in Librarianship at University College, London. With his wife, Helen, he created a comprehensive careers information classification system.

Tomlinson would stay with CRAC for 16 years, during which time his responsibilities widened to include the key role of editing the growing list of comprehensive guides to the entire UK education system. In the

In 1967 this 32-page 'users manual' for CRAC's new Careers Indexing and Retrieval System was published, funded by CYEE.

February 1967 volume of *The Library Association Record*, he wrote that:

'*An efficient library service is vital – development and innovation for CRAC must mean development and innovation for the library…The information and library services are so closely intertwined that it is not possible (nor advisable) to differentiate between them.*'

In 1965 CRAC started a new course, 'Careers Library on a Shoestring', in which teachers were trained on how best to set up their own libraries. Trainees were presented with a list compiled by CRAC of key titles required by even the most basic careers library. The list was subdivided into titles for girls and boys, each strand totalling to an outlay of around £10. The package offered a practical and realisable answer to a problem that had dogged schools throughout the country.

By the summer of 1966 James Tomlinson and his team had devised a completely new careers information indexing system, with syllabic (as opposed to numeric) notation, and had indexed and classified the CRAC Library's 10,000 documents and publications. Another 5,000 items were integrated by the following summer. A punched-card 'Peek-a-Boo' topic search system was put in place following consultation with a number of librarians. In 1967 the Central Youth Employment Executive approached CRAC to seek permission to use the new indexing and retrieval system for a publication which would be issued jointly by CYEE and CRAC. This was agreed, and the slightly amended version of CRAC's CLIC – now renamed CLCI – was sent to all secondary schools and YEOs free of charge.

CLIC/CLCI sorted publications into twenty-six main classification groups covering broad areas, which were then split into a range of subheadings. For instance, the 'Entertainment and Recreation' classification '*G*' was subdivided into: '*Drama*' – *Gab*; '*Music*' – *Gad*; '*Dancing*' – *Gag*; '*Broadcasting*' – *Gal*; and '*Film Work*' – *Gam*. To make it easier to remember the classifications, Tomlinson exploited the syllabic notation system, taking the opportunity for some private jokes, e.g. '*Teaching*'- *Fab*; '*Medicine and Surgery*'- *Jab*; '*Local Government Professional*' – *Dad*; and '*Accountancy*' - *Nab*. A comprehensive alphabetical index listed some 500 careers and education subjects showing their relevant classifications. The associated Card Index was described as '*an easy source of reference to all documents stored under the scheme and an up-to-date comprehensive bibliography of careers and further and higher education literature*'. On the recommendation of the British Council, the Cambridge office received visits from Israel's Vocational Guidance Research Unit, Malta's Department of Labour and Emigration, the Swedish Ministry of Labour and the Thai Ministry of

Education, principally to learn more about the workings of the library system.

Learning Quickly

CRAC made rapid advances in its first two years, under difficult financial circumstances. Any social enterprise must be prepared for rough times, particularly in its infancy, but with no shareholder investors CRAC had had to learn quickly. Responsive and eager to learn, it rapidly recognised where it was most needed and how it could be most effective. At the same time, its management realised that without an economic framework with clear plans, forecasts and budgets, the organisation could not survive.

5
Consolidation

The CRAC *Report* of July 1966 starkly indicated both very rapid growth and the problems that this had created:

'Whilst revenue has risen sharply, this has been matched by greatly increased revenue expenditure.'

All of the UK's 3,100 schools with sixth forms now received at least one CRAC service or publication, the number of subscribing schools stood at 2,000 and teachers from 600 different schools had attended CRAC courses during the year. The Profit and Loss Account showed an operating loss of just £177, the Foundation Fund Appeal having raised the necessary balances to pay for operational costs not covered by the fees and subscriptions earned from the various publications and courses. With an expanded staff of 25, conditions in the St Andrews Street office were becoming impossibly cramped and inconvenient and further expansion into new premises would soon be an added cost burden. Nonetheless, CRAC continued to be a beacon of innovation.

Making Movies

Despite the acknowledged need for more scientists, technologists and engineers in the economy, as alluded to in Harold Wilson's 'White Heat' speech of 1963, there was evidence of a worrying lack of interest in science subjects among school pupils. The years following the Robbins Report saw a percentage rise in arts student numbers (from 40% of all full-time university students in 1961–62 to 44% in 1966–67) but a decline in pure science students (from 25.4% in 1961–62 to 24.1% in 1966–67). For many pupils what they were taught in the school science laboratory seemed to bear little relevance to real life and this restricted the number that decided to pursue sciences at a higher level. CRAC saw the problem and correctly guessed that it might be able to get industrial sponsorship for projects or materials which would open up ways to change pupils' attitudes in this respect.

Such a possibility arose when Bridgewater visited Kim Taylor, the headmaster of Sevenoaks School, to meet one of his science teachers, Gerd Sommerhoff. Sommerhoff had started a high-tech workshop where pupils were helped to work out and apply the physics, chemistry or

Sevenoaks goes on the screen

An enterprising move by the Careers Research and Advisory Centre in Cambridge was brought to a climax in the theatre of the Shell Centre, London, recently, when a distinguished audience, including Mr. Basil de Ferranti, the head of ICT, watched a preview of a film called Creativity in School.

What CRAC has done, with the admirable help of Mithras Films Ltd. and the modest assistance of this journal, is to make a film of the Technical Activities Centre, founded and run by Mr. Gerd Sommerhoff at Sevenoaks. During its thirty minutes, the film explains the philosophy of the Centre, shows some of the work that has been achieved, and records the views of boys and masters. The film had a warm reception, including a tribute from the school's headmaster, Mr. L. C. Taylor. It may soon be given a wide viewing on television.

Mr Gerd Sommerhoff does not solve his pupils' problems for them, but he may, as he does here, direct their problem solving strategy

A boy at the centre explains to the audience some of the problems involved in his project

An older student consults with an industrialist over a problem which has arisen with the use of a transistor in the echo-device he is contriving as an aid

Stills from CRAC's first documentary film *Creativity in School, New Education,* March 1966.

biology principles involved in a wide range of projects that interested them. Pupils' projects ranged from determining how bats function using sonar with very limited vision, to the principles of hovercraft and helicopter flight. This work had enhanced performance in classroom results and attracted more students to stick with these subjects at A-level whilst opening their minds to a much wider range of degree course options. The project was an approach to the *'practical, realistic and vocational'* teaching recommended in the Newsom Report of 1963, but for A-level pupils it had the further advantage of awakening interest in non-school degree courses in the applied sciences including engineering and biotechnology.

A film about Sommerhoff's project could disseminate this important new work. With the enthusiastic support of both Sommerhoff and Taylor, Bridgewater set about finding and briefing a film director and securing sponsorship. Six companies, including Shell, donated two-thirds of the production costs; the final third was to be covered by sales and hiring fees (it was hired 172 times in its first year). *Creativity in School*, a 30-minute documentary, was premiered in March 1966 at the 300-seat Shell Centre in London. Promoted by the Ministry of Technology and the CBI, the film was shown widely in schools and colleges of education, received a special screening at the British Association for the Advancement of Science and was featured in BBC's *Tomorrow's World* (its prime-time science programme).

Creativity in School made a small surplus and a major impact. It was therefore decided to embark on a series of six CRAC *Perspective* films, all with the overall objective:

'to describe not just the type of work done in the particular field of employment but also the characteristics and qualities of the employees themselves.'

The first was *Computer People,* followed by *Marketing People, Production People, Personnel People, Finance People*, and *Research and Development People. A Facts Book* describing specific entry qualifications and training opportunities was provided with each film, which was distributed free (on written request) to schools, colleges and universities whilst other clients could hire or buy it. The films were released between 1968 and 1971. Reviewing *Computer People* for the *Financial Times* in January 1969, John Chittock wrote:

'I rate Computer People *as one of the best films I have seen in the last 12 months. It is a probing documentary investigation…'*

Creativity in School was a classic example of how CRAC identified a need—often emerging from informal conversations with contacts in

Of Low Degree

By LESLIE ADRIAN

FOR what commodity does demand exceed supply by two to one, and yet leave lots over and to spare? Answer: higher education. The *Daily Mail* survey of university places and applicants came up with the first figure. I found the surplus in an advertisement from the Department of Education headed 'Advice to students seeking a degree course this year.' A craftily worded ad., it went on: 'There are vacancies at nearly 120 centres of further education in various parts of the country. Courses leading to degrees of the Council for National Academic Awards or to external London degrees, and courses leading to Higher National Diplomas, are available. . . .' Yes, the hard sell is for places in educational institutions of low degree, and on the whole the young idea does not want to know.

What he does want to know is the sort of course listed in Pelican Books' *University Choice?* This 7s. 6d. tome offers an Ariadne's thread through the labyrinth built of generations of neglect, expediency and selfish empire-building by remote and all too effectual dons. The introduction to Klaus Boehm's educational encyclopaedia contains the heartlessness of the matter. 'Nobody who qualifies for a university place ought to be prevented from taking it up through lack of funds. The state sees to that. Effectively, most of the more intellectually gifted members of a generation have the opportunity to define their social status [huh?]. Nevertheless a degree in a non-vocational subject . . . is not necessarily a passport to professional status, a qualification sufficient unto itself.' My huh.

So, under 'Law' we are then told that the law taught at university (for three whole years, mind you) is not designed for lawyers, and that half of those who read law fail to go on into practice. The book does not say why, but we all know the tale of the Oxford law graduate who could not get his solicitor's finals. There seems to be a complacent air about the calm acceptance that even now, under all our modern pressures, a university education is not intended to equip the recipient to do a job.

The Warwick University mathematician is more sympathetic, with general advice on the importance of following one's enthusiasm rather than setting out to seek vocational training, and to centre study on one subject rather than a number. But the impression inevitably carried away from this collection of academic copywriting is of confusion. 'Some universities treat "Honours" as a description of a kind of course. . . . Others use it to describe a level of accomplishment. . . .' Every subject, every course, every university department appears to have a

different approach to botany, *Beowulf* and bimetallism. The odd thing is that all the attempts to catalogue and codify this particularly private kind of public enterprise have been private.

The biggest and probably the best shopping list is Cornmarket Press's *Which University?* (21s.). In this compendium, without frills, they put the bare facts about the courses available and some useful stuff about the living facilities at the various colleges, even down to LSE's consultant psychiatrist. There is a useful note on the use of the University Central Council on Admissions, the clearing house that has saved so much multiple applying for places. Harping on the hope springs eternal theme, the text says 'It may tell you that you cannot be accepted. This is a *rejection*.'

But with all those vacancies about, most young folk should be able to find a niche somewhere. *Which University?* has increased its revenue and its scope by having a paid section on what they so politely term 'The Colleges,' a bunch of technical colleges who have bought space, the Colleges of Advanced Technology having, thanks to Robbins, been gathered into the body of the work. The third in the trinity of helpers of those plotting their way through to the first session at Heaven-knows-where College to read God-knows-what is the Careers Research Advisory Centre at 25 St Andrews Street, Cambridge. They have recently produced a series of leaflets on the various courses in each subject that each university offers. Some of the comparisons are revealing. But what baffles an old taxpayer like me is why, with all the millions we've been pouring into education, we have been happy till now to let it all happen at random.

The ad. from the Ministry shouts about 'Up-to-the-minute information about vacancies . . . available in August and September from your local education authority, which has been invited to appoint a local advisory officer. The earlier you apply, the wider your choice.' There's an opportunity for somebody.

Reproduced from the *Spectator,* 29 July 1966.

both the education and employer fields—and sought to identify and disseminate innovative solutions. There had been no co-ordinated call for *Creativity in School* by teachers; rather, the problem was detected by the CRAC team. The film highlighted a problem and offered a solution, of which teachers were then eager to take advantage. As CRAC produced more services (whether films, publications or courses), increased demand was generated from the education sector—both at university and non-university level—as teachers recognised the innovative nature of the material offered. For instance, the publication of the *CBI Card Index* resulted in over 100 letters of thanks from schools in its first year. In these still early days of serious attention to careers education and guidance, CRAC was not responding to specific demands but identifying the needs which would create that demand.

Growing the Publishing Programme

A commentator writing under the name of Astryx wrote in the *Times Educational Supplement* in March 1968 that:

'Some of the most sensible remarks made nowadays are to be found in the publications of the Careers Research and Advisory Centre.'

Subject teachers needed to assimilate a wealth of new information on an ongoing basis, including information about unfamiliar non-school subjects like the American History courses offered by several new universities and the whole range of Engineering courses. In response, CRAC relaunched its most important publishing project, the *Course Comparisons*, now renamed and branded as the *CRAC Degree Course Guides*, with 46 titles.

The Department of Education and Science directed readers to the *Degree Course Guides* in its own *Signposts to Higher Education,* and good relations between the Department and CRAC were further reflected in the exchange of speakers at the organisations' respective conferences and courses on access to higher education. Each *Guide* had some 40 pages and around 2,000 copies of each were sold, mainly to schools, in a twelve-month period. Each title was written by an academic in the particular subject, and was fully updated every other year (with a *Digest of Changes* published in the interim). Leslie Adrian wrote in praise of the series in the *Spectator*:

'What baffles an old taxpayer like me is why, with all the millions we've been pouring into education, we have been happy till now to let it all [the choosing of university courses] happen at random.'

All relevant degree-awarding bodies in the country were consulted in the compilation of the *Degree Course Guides*, which built ties between

How to woo the undergraduates

BY CHARLES RAW

FOR THE PAST ten days some 60 undergraduates about to start their last year at university have been put through a rigorous introduction to life in industry in a Summer School course at Oxford. The course, the first of its kind, was organised by the Careers Research and Advisory Council and the Urwick Management Centre: it represents probably the first serious attempt to woo brighter undergraduates away from the atractions of academic life or the prestige of a career in the civil service.

To do the persuading and incidentally paying all the expenses through their firms—were 30 young graduates who had already opted for a business career and had been with their firms, mostly big ones, for from just one year to a dozen or so. The aim was, by getting the two sides sitting together at lectures and working together on case studies to give the undergraduates a realistic idea of what choosing an industrial career really involved.

The undergraduates came from universities throughout the country. They were chosen through tutors and appointments boards as potential first or good second class degrees. In the closing days the organisers carried out a brief survey into the undergraduates reactions: 94 per cent. said that the course had helped them to make a decision on their future careers. The results of the survey went on to show that 48 per cent. had decided to go into large companies while only 16 per cent. wanted to join small companies.

Together with the few who had fixed on a career with the nationalised industries, a total of 68 per cent. said they had decided on a career in industry. However, after talking to a selection, it was clear that a high proportion of participants had decided before the course. What the survey did not reveal was whether any of the 30 odd per cent. remaining had actively been discouraged from going into industry as a result of the course. I spoke only to one, a sociologist from East Anglia who said he had been put off.

"The graduates tend to take the lead in most of the discussions," A. H. D. Barrow a tutor from Henley Staff College told me. This was borne out by a brief visit to one of the sessions. But some graduates felt differently: "I reckon the undergraduates contribute as much in areas where we have no specialised knowledge" a Shell executive said. The graduates were not there to recruit but, as potential personnel directors, they were interested to find out the reactions of undergraduates to the course.

Reproduced from the *Sunday Times,* 12 September 1966.

CRAC and the universities. CRAC also undertook the distribution to schools of several universities' prospectuses. Universities regularly provided speakers at CRAC conferences, especially those aimed at improving teachers' knowledge of non-school subjects to pass on to their degree course candidates. For instance, the Vice-Chancellors of Leeds, Glasgow, Heriot-Watt and Bath all participated in CRAC courses in 1966.

Other important publications included, in May 1966, *Which B.Ed*, the first comprehensive guide to the recently introduced Bachelor of Education degree for secondary school teachers. The single most widely purchased publication was *Students in Transition* which annually updated the outcome of Watts's study of students' activities during the year-long 'gap' between leaving school and university.

The Undergraduate Summer Schools

In September 1966 CRAC ran its first 'Undergraduate Summer School' at University College, Oxford. The School was the idea of Michael Butterwick, a founder member of CRAC's Council, and its programme was designed by Butterwick and Bridgewater working with management consultants Urwick Orr and Partners. It was a ten-day residential course aiming to help undergraduates understand how their degree course studies would be relevant to particular jobs in industry and commerce and to consider such a career route.

Case studies were commissioned to portray the British working environment. For instance, the first financial case study was based around the case *'G' Plan Furniture* and was written by two merchant bankers, David Berryman and John Swallow, who had been directly involved. Another case study was based on the Hotpoint electricals company, which had appeared on paper to be profitable but had suddenly got into difficulties. Many of the early tutors had done postgraduate Business Administration Courses in the North American and French business schools and were well equipped to demonstrate the intellectual challenges of industrial decision making.

The December 1966 house journal of Fisons, one of the companies who co-operated with the project, commented:

'...*at a time when world competition, technological change and our general economy makes it vital that industry should attract the very best recruits...numerous graduates are dismissing industry from their plans without knowing anything about it.*'

The CRAC courses were based around five UK-relevant case studies and a Business Game devised by IBM. The key ingredient was the

The first job after university

University appointments boards do a very useful job in bringing potential employers into contact with potential graduate employees. Lord Heyworth thinks that they could do a still better job if there were more of them, better paid, backed by bigger staffs and better offices, and by some kind of central organisation able to store and distribute as required information too detailed to be conveniently circulated throughout the system. In this view—set out in his report published today—he is surely right, and perhaps the statistical analysis which was conducted on too narrow a basis was hardly needed to illuminate his finding. In the last twenty-five years the work of the appointments boards has both increased in bulk and become more complex as more kinds of employer have come to use them. Their resources have not kept pace with the demands made on them.

They have to carry in any case a heavy load of stored information. The central unit which Lord Heyworth suggests would lighten their load by carrying a good deal of it for them, at call when required. There is likely to be a good deal ascertainable about the requirements of particular employers which cannot effectively be supplied in full to all boards, but which should be obtainable at short notice. The central unit might, for instance, maintain specialists on the needs of particular industries or public services, on which appointments boards could call when considering whether a student was a likely candidate for work in that field. It is worth considering whether this central unit could also serve the newly founded Careers, Research, and Advisory Centre which exists to advise careers teachers, and through them senior boys and girls at schools, about prospects of employment for which they may wish to prepare themselves, whether or not they think of going into the work directly or after a period of higher education.

Lord Heyworth suggests that the universities should be prepared to spend more on their appointments boards. There is a strong case for doing so. But is there any good reason why employers should not also contribute something in respect of work which the boards do for them? It is clearly of great help to an employer to be able to ask for a dozen or so promising candidates, acquainted with his general requirements, to be assembled for his consideration. To get that far by his own efforts would cost a good deal. Why should not employers, saying how many candidates they would like to interview, pay a small fee for each one put before them as an applicant worth considering?

Reproduced from the *Guardian*, 25 June 1964.

Making Better Careers Decisions

An entirely new way of helping undergraduates to make realistic careers decisions has been developed by the Careers Research and Advisory Centre in Cambridge. Over 60 undergraduates have just reported back to the centre after attending a summer school in Oxford where they spent 12 days studying every aspect of management, engaging in detailed case study projects and dipping into statistics and operations research. Alongside the undergraduates were young graduate executives.

This meant that not only could the undergraduates learn about industry formally through high-level lectures and discussions but they were able to hear the views of people closer to themselves in age and experience. First reports are that the scheme has fully justified CRAC's hopes. A high percentage of undergraduates say they have been helped to make career decisions, and the centre's new course will become a regular feature of the careers landscape. The next summer school will attempt to cater for 300 undergraduates and will be held at Nottingham University.

The programme was carefully designed by the Urwick Management Centre. A total of 22 lectures covered management in production, finance, personnel and sales departments as well as network analysis, group motivation, trade unions and the work of the Glacier Institute.

Many of the undergraduates feel they are probably committed to industry because they are studying subjects like economics, engineering or geography. They were therefore particularly anxious to get a clearer idea of the functions of management. They said that the course provided this. Mr. R. P. Kirchner, studying geography at Swansea, said the value of the course was in letting people sample industry, not at managing director level but at the level of the brand manager. Several people said the managing director image of industry was not helpful as only a minority would ever reach that position. Mr. K. Hillman, training with an international firm, said most of the undergraduates wanted a down-to-earth description of what people did in particular jobs from day to day.

The course was not an exercise to persuade people to enter industry, but an attempt to provide facts and people so that the students could assess both. Some executives explained that their firms had expressly told them not to try to sell their firms to the students. However, over three-quarters of the students have decided to consider entering industry.

A few students derived a different benefit from the course. They decided not to enter firms. The main point made by the dissenting students was that the talks they heard put everything on a profit basis. They wanted to know whether firms had a responsibility to society or whether companies were mechanisms.

Whatever views students have formed, the CRAC project has helped them to clear their minds on one of the most important decisions they will ever have to make. A means for frequent and regular exchange between industry and the student world has now been established.

Reproduced from the *Sunday Times*, 12 September 1966.

involvement of young graduates already at work, whose experience was essential for realistic discussion in small groups and for solutions of the case-study problems. Some 20 graduates were sponsored by their employers to work alongside 64 students in their penultimate year of study. As the *Times Review of Industry* noted:

'*Mr. K Hillman, training with an international firm, said most of the undergraduates wanted a down-to-earth description of what people did in particular jobs from day to day.*'

The school was designed to be residential, with time deliberately allocated for informal, bar-time conversations between the already employed graduates and the undergraduates. In *Management Today,* Martin Sorrell wrote that the course was '*welcomed as an eye-opener by the undergraduates*'. The *Times Review of Industry* said:

'*A means for frequent and regular exchange between industry and the student world has now been established.*'

Building on this success, three further Summer Schools were held in July 1967 (two at the University of Nottingham and one at the University of Edinburgh), catering for 300 students in all. Undergraduates were charged a fee of around £5, small enough to be affordable but large enough to make sure they were serious about the course. Industrial participants were charged a sponsoring fee which was considerably more and contributed to the overall costs. These Summer Schools '*really put CRAC on the map*' in the world of graduate recruitment, most of its earlier efforts having been concentrated on secondary schools.

Research activities geared toward graduate careers included a survey of the growing importance of languages in industry and another on the natural wastage of arts graduates. An investigation looking at the career prospects of women in education exemplified the attitudes of the sixties. Of 158 major employers approached, only 30 said they would employ female technologists and scientists, 40 said they would take female arts graduates but 88 reported that they only wanted male graduates.

Establishing a Scottish Office

In September 1966 a regional office for Scotland was opened in Edinburgh, with Ian Thompson as Director, funded by Scottish contributions to the Foundation Appeal. Scotland's education system being separate from that in England and Wales—particularly its Higher exams as opposed to A-levels—the new office enabled CRAC to respond to specifically Scottish needs. The first-year focus was on planning and organising a residential course for 80 Scottish school teachers at Edinburgh University and then building relationships with the contacts

Swann-song at Oxford

An eight-day summer school, designed as a first step
to bridge the gap between academic research and industry,
ended last Thursday at University College, Oxford

Take one hundred variegated, unblemished PhD
students, all two-thirds of the way to their virgin-
pure doctorates. Add forty-odd cynical PhDs
from industry, whose theses probably lie gathering
dust on the tops of wardrobes in their semis
while they do daily battle with the tawdry, real
world of men and machine. Deposit the lot into
the 17th century surroundings of a peaceful
Oxford college in summer. Season with a liberal
sprinkling of bright, sharp catalysts from the
half-world of academic business teaching. Thicken
slightly with a sober selection of top industrialists.
Keep the mixture on the boil furiously for 13
hours a day for eight days. The result? A dish,
"brilliant and rather anarchical", according to
a *Times* correspondent, that should at least have
the flavour of a promising *hors-d'oeuvre* to
Professor Michael Swann and others concerned
with the persisting and widening gulf between the
rarified atmosphere of university research and the
down-to-earth pragmatism of industry.

Paragraph 42 of the Interim Report of the
Working Group on Manpower Parameters for
Scientific Growth (the Swann Committee Report),
published last October, pinpointed the "widespread belief" amongst PhD students, "that academic research is the only respectable outcome of a
scientific education". One of the readers of the
report whose eye was struck by this phrase was
Klaus Boehm, the director of the Careers Research
and Advisory Centre (CRAC), an independent
non-profit making organization set up in 1964
as an information unit to link the fields of education and employment. Hitherto concerned mainly
with the sixth form, CRAC got together with the
Science Research Council and between them arose
the idea for a summer school to introduce second
year postgraduate science and technology students
receiving an SRC grant, drawn from all universities, "to the many types of industrial and administrative problems and some of the techniques used
in solving them".

The course was evolved from discussions
between CRAC and the London Business School.
Designed with a view to making the maximum use
of participative methods of teaching, it was decided
to get the message of the course over in two ways.
On the one hand by an intensive programme of case

histories, exercises, lectures and a business game. On
the other hand by mixing up the students with
PhD scientists currently attached to industry and
research establishments, so that by working in teams
and holding informal discussion, the students would
acquire concrete information on the life of PhDs
outside the walls of the university.

Earlier this year the SRC circularized those of its
students at the relevant stage of their doctorates.
The response was encouraging, there being over
300 applications for the 100 available places. A
selection was made in order to obtain a fair balance
from different disciplines and universities; in the
event, the school consisted of 34 physicists, 16
biologists, 12 mathematicians, 12 chemists, 13
engineers and 13 others from an assortment of
subjects. The response from industry was, predictably,
less enthusiastic: of the "Times 300" companies only
a handful nominated course members. Companies
from the science-orientated industries, such as ICI
and Unilever, were well represented; smaller manufacturing industries, scarcely at all. PhDs from
government laboratories were virtually non-existent,
though the nationalized industries were thinly represented. Of the hoped-for 50 PhDs, 42 were
present.

The pace of the course was intense. The mornings,
from 9.00 to 12.30, were devoted to the study of
case histories of firms (several of which were torn to
shreds in discussion), informal lectures on topics such
as operational research, systems analysis and so on,
and to exercises such as the one entitled "In-Tray".
In this, the student found himself in the hair-raising
position of being suddenly promoted, in the character
of one Harry Paulson, from being district manager
of a small branch of a firm called Wrights Business
Forms, Inc., to being manager of a large and thriving
branch of the same firm in London. He finds a pile
of papers in his in-tray on arriving at his new London
office, and has just $1\frac{1}{2}$ hours to take decisions on
them all—with no secretary to tell him what to do!

The afternoons were spent in the preparation of
these cases and exercises, with a tutor (the majority
of whom were lecturers from the Mechanical
Engineering Department, Imperial College) on hand if
needed. After dinner each evening a more formal
lecture was delivered by a guest speaker.

Graham Chedd
assistant science editor

Reproduced from *New Scientist,* 21 September 1967.

that arose from it. In its first month in Scotland the Scottish Ministry of Labour invited CRAC to address its conference for careers advisers. In July 1967 the first 'Summer School for Scottish Undergraduates' took place.

In 1968 the Scottish Education Department published *Guidance to Scottish Secondary Schools*, which called for interlinked guidance in three fields: curricular, vocational and personal. In response CRAC set about instituting staff training schemes, developing resource materials and devising systems 'consistent with varying local conditions'.

Introducing the Graduate Schools

Dr Duncan Davis, ICI's Director of Research who had been involved as a speaker at one of the first undergraduate Summer Schools and who was also the Industrial Representative on the Science Research Council, suggested to Bridgewater that, as a response to the upcoming Swann Report's findings on the difficulty of attracting graduate scientists to industry, CRAC might develop a special School for postgraduate science students. A quote in the Swann Report described a *'widespread belief'* among PhD students that *'academic research is the only respectable outcome of a scientific education.'*

By now Klaus Boehm was working full-time for CRAC, having turned down the opportunity of a college post in favour of the chance to be active in a vital market and attracted by the energy emanating out of CRAC. Following a number of discussions Bridgewater had decided to take a risk and, without budget or funding, had employed Boehm as a salaried Research Projects Director charged with strategically expanding the CRAC portfolio. The essence of this decision was that, as with the ACE Conference which he had organised in 1963, Boehm would be able to generate sufficient revenue from new projects to support his own salary costs. Looking back on his decision to leave academe, he explained that he *'joined CRAC because it was an effective business in a vital market'*. Boehm brought with him a rigorous intellect and a significant address book of university and industrial contacts.

The project proposed by Davis was immediately given to Boehm and the first *Graduate School* programme was developed with the advice of Professor Tommy Wilson, who was directing the Sloan programme at the London Business School, working closely with Dr Geoffrey Potter, a Research Officer at the SRC. Wilson (whose career was to include roles as a professor of brain surgery, founding fellow of the London Business School, founding secretary of the Royal College of GPs, a founder of the Tavistock Institute and an adviser on the social sciences

ARTICLE REPRINTED FROM-

THE TIMES

Thursday September 14, 1967

Integrating the PhDs

A brilliant, rather anarchial summer school comes to an end at University College, Oxford, today. It was organized by the Careers Research and Advisory Centre, and the Science Research Council, with the purpose of bringing together Ph.D. scientists working in universities and industry.

The school was inspired by the highlighting in the Swann Committee Report of industry's difficulty in attracting graduate scientists. C.R.A.C. and S.R.C. decided jointly that a move in the right direction would be to bring together Ph.D. post-graduate students working in science and technology in universities with Ph.D. graduates now working in industry and commerce.

As a result 100 university men —320 applied—and 42 from industry and commerce arrived in Oxford early last week for the £10,000, nine-day course, and with the exception of the first and last days, and last Sunday, the students worked a 13-hour day.

Admitting that the school, by virtue of its objective, was to a large extent an experiment, the organizers agreed that it would be hard to positively evaluate its effect. There was a certain amount of natural segregation between the men from industry and the university scientists. Although the latter seemed reluctant to turn their faces from the pseudo-monastic purity of their lives in University laboratories, they rather shyly agreed that the school had added a new and favourable perspective to their attitude towards a career in industry.

Part of this change of attitude can be put down to the system of teaching adopted, which was to encourage the maximum student participation in lectures. And some iconoclastic attitudes of the lecturers no doubt helped.

"Their is an attitude that debt is wicked. Some firms are proud that there is not a pound of debt on their balance sheet. My answer to that is sack the financial director", was an example from Professor H. B. Rose, Professor of Finance at the London Business School, which relaxed the atmosphere during his lectures on discounted cash flow concepts.

Throughout the course a running Business Game, based on the Game developed by Imperial College, was played daily, and may well prove to have been one of the most valuable features of the school. Within a few days the pure scientists were happily chattering away in business jargon, and thinking in terms of problems effecting profit oriented operations, even if towards the end of the school some of the "companies" of five students were heading inexorably towards bankruptcy.

About midway through the game the students were asked to complete a questionnaire on their group and the allocation of roles. The analysis of the answers could provide the key to the value of the school.

Printed for TIMES NEWSPAPERS LIMITED, London, E.C.4, England, by
THE BRADBURY AGNEW PRESS LTD.

to the board of Unilever) suggested bringing in Charles Handy (one of the co-founders of the London Business School) to help design and then direct the first School. The detailed programme was designed along broadly similar lines to the Undergraduate Schools, but with new case-study material and a new business game.

The first Graduate School took place in September 1967 at University College, Oxford. Specialist industrial managers acted as tutors to guide discussion groups. The School was attended by 100 research students whose fees and costs were fully paid by the SRC, and by 30 young managers from industry and the public sector holding scientific doctorates, whose employers paid an economic fee. Among the first group of young industrialists was Callum McCarthy, a post-doctoral recruit with ICI who would later head up the Financial Services Authority, and Ray Dolby, who would turn his Cambridge PhD thesis on sound reproduction into a hugely successful business.

Handy later recalled the first delegates taking part in a game based on a simplified model of society where business, workers, their unions, the public sector and the government were all competing for scarce resources. At one point, one of the groups of students 'kidnapped' Handy himself and demanded a ransom from the other groups for his release! David Blandford, one of the course tutors and CRAC's future Director, remembered '*the excitement and stimulation of the new way of learning that the Graduate Schools represented*' and how the enthusiasm of the young managers was conveyed to the PhD students '*almost by osmosis*'.

The *Times* described the first School as '*brilliant and rather anarchical*' whilst the *New Statesman* called it:

'*...a promising hors-d'oeuvre to Professor Michael Swann and others concerned with the persisting and widening gulf between the rarified atmosphere of university research and the down-to-earth pragmatism of industry.*'

The SRC awarded CRAC a contract to run five courses a year. Forty years on, the Graduate Schools remain a cornerstone of the CRAC programme, embedded both within universities' own support for research students and run nationally by CRAC within the VITAE programme funded by Research Councils UK, led and managed by CRAC and delivered in partnership with regional hubs hosted by universities.

Accommodating Rapid Expansion

In July 1967 the audited statement of accounts showed a year-on-year doubling of CRAC's total income, whilst the profit and loss account

PRESS

Science Research Counci

STATE HOUSE · HIGH HOLBORN · LONDON · W.C.1 · TELEPHONE: CHANCERY 1262

April 10, 1967

SCIENCE RESEARCH COUNCIL TO SPONSOR ONE HUNDRED RESEARCH STUDENTS

AT CRAC GRADUATE SUMMER SCHOOL, UNIVERSITY COLLEGE, OXFORD

The Science Research Council intends to sponsor one hundred of its research students at an intensive eight day residential summer school which will serve as an introduction to administrative concepts and techniques. The school will be held at University College, Oxford, from September 6 - 14, 1967, and in addition to research students there will be fifty Ph.D.s from industry, commerce and the public services, both scientists and technologists. The course has been arranged by the Careers Research and Advisory Centre at Cambridge which is already well known for its undergraduate summer schools and its higher education information services to universities and schools. The programme has been devised in association with the London Business School and Mr. R. D. James, Director (Elect), of the Executive Development Programme will be Director of Studies at the course.

Its objectives are to introduce postgraduate students to many different administrative problems which exist in industry and government service and the techniques used to solve them; to show that these problems, while different from those encountered in academic research, are intellectually challenging and demanding; to assist students in their choice of career by showing them industrial and administrative activities and informing them of techniques that will be of use in making their own academic research more efficient.

Case work will be a predominant feature and students will work in groups of ten under the guidance of a tutor. Lectures will be given and a business game played. The five themes of the course will be:

/The organisation's

Reproduced extract from SRC Press Release, 10 April 1967.

reported a small operating surplus. From its unsteady financial position in 1964, CRAC had established a reasonable financial position in just three years, reflecting '*the ability of the education and employment systems to respond to innovation at a time when precise needs in this field had scarcely been expressed*'.

The staff had now grown to 35 including a newly appointed Keele graduate, Claire Bosanquet, who was brought in as a full-time University Liaison Officer. There is an indication of the pragmatism and absence of pretension demanded of staff members in a recruitment advertisement that year:

'*The sales manager of the Careers Research and Advisory Centre needs another pair of hands—sorry, we meant a modern sales and marketing executive.*'

CRAC's offices were now spread through three adjoining buildings in St Andrews Street and the Scottish office. In addition the formidable Miss E.C. (Betty) Bather, who had been a supporter of CRAC from her position as a Personnel Manager for Courtaulds, was recruited to run a CRAC Schools Liaison Office covering South Western England.

Schools' feedback on the *CBI Card Index* had suggested the system was becoming unwieldy and CRAC therefore proposed to the CBI that the *Index* be published in book form. The *Careers Index Cards* and a selection of CRAC *Information Bulletins* were incorporated into a *Yearbook,* to which two more volumes covering further education and graduate careers were later added.

Extending the Reach

CRAC's 1967 *Statement of Principal Activities* stated that:

'*This process, through which each person must ultimately find a place in the world of work, starts at a very early age and continues all the way through school and college and into employment.*'

One of CRAC's editors, Richard Slessor, wrote whilst reviewing CRAC's early years that:

'*...a large part of our work during our first three years has been aimed at the sixth-form level. This was not deliberate policy so much as a response to need.*'

A key step in meeting the information needs of younger people was taken in 1967 with the publication of *Middle School Choice*, the '*first CRAC publication for the younger pupil*'. Its author, Michael Smith, then the Deputy Headmaster of Hartcliffe School and later the first head of Filton High School (both in Bristol), had for some time been providing his pupils aged 13 and 14 with information sheets to assist in making their CSE and O-level choices. Bridgewater saw the potential in collating and developing these sheets into a book and approached Smith with the idea. Smith compiled the first edition with Susan Minay of CRAC as his editor. It sold 12,000 copies within six months of publication and was revised and updated annually for several subsequent years (see p.78).

Over the next few years Smith developed a number of record systems for his own school, which were then prepared for wider use by CRAC. The CRAC *Subject Assessment System* was developed by him to collect pupils' reports from individual subject teachers, replacing the single sheet report form on which teachers could be influenced by colleagues' comments. Another CRAC/Smith product, the *Careers Record System,* offered a way of tracing each pupil's development, including achievements, vocational preferences and details of careers interviews.

On the advice of Council member A.J. Caston, now Head of Careers at Sussex University, the *Connolly Occupational Interests Questionnaire* was published in 1967. In the course of his work Caston had noticed a correlation between personal interest and success (or lack thereof) in particular degree courses. The *Connolly Questionnaire* had been developed using British occupational groupings to assist careers advisers to identify the relative strengths of a student's interests and Caston had used it to advise pupils on their degree course choices. CRAC created a *User's Handbook* and a course for careers advisers on using the *Questionnaire.* This was followed in 1970 by the *Crowley Occupational Interests Blank*, designed for use with younger pupils to get them to start thinking about future plans. Crowley was a creative YEO who worked with pupils with no expectation of going to university and he suggested that CRAC might publish the *Interests Blank.*

By now around 2,000 students, teachers, employers, careers advisers and personnel officers were attending CRAC courses and conferences annually. Courses included 'Turn or Return to Teaching', established in response to the introduction of the B.Ed teaching qualification; and 'The Retention of Engineering and Science Graduates in British Industry', at which Gerald Fowler, Joint Parliamentary Secretary at the Ministry of Technology, presented a paper. The latter course was a further response to the Swann Report and its concern about the shortage of science graduates going into Industry. In response to the Swann findings, CRAC undertook a high-profile research project into unfilled places at technical colleges and another into the favoured careers of sixth formers.

Meanwhile, the CBI and CRAC organised courses for teachers aimed at equipping them with the knowledge and techniques to teach 'An Introduction to Business' to sixth formers, because Business Studies was now entering the curriculum of a growing number of schools. Another programme of courses for teachers exploring the relationships between school subjects and non-school subject degree courses covered both science-based and arts subjects and was heavily over-subscribed. This programme included, for example, a three-day course for heads of History departments developed by John Chancellor, managing director of Sidgwick & Jackson, whose publications included a 'partwork', *History Makers*, edited by William Armstrong (father of internationally renowned singer Dido). Speakers included John Thorn (Headmaster of Winchester College), Robert Jackson (who later, as Under-Secretary of State for Higher Education, was involved in the final decisions about ECCTIS — see Chapter 8) and Graham Howes (Director of Studies in Social and Political Sciences at Trinity Hall, Cambridge).

Mike Leonard, who served as President of the National Association of Careers and Guidance Teachers, recalled:

'I started as a teacher with responsibility for careers in 1968. At that time the only organisation that was providing anything for work in schools was CRAC. The real emphasis on their courses were practical considerations for the classroom. What can you actually do? What materials have you got and how can you use them? As well as keeping up-to-date with the many changes that were coming in from the various governments... CRAC was the one that in my experience careers teachers went for because you could rely on the materials. They had been written by practitioners, by people who knew what they were talking about.'

The Interviewing Skills Programme

The 'Undergraduate Summer School' had thrown up an interesting new problem, not specifically dealt within its programme, concerning the interviewing skills—or lack of them—of industrial managers trying to recruit graduates. To air this problem CRAC developed and organised a Winter Conference for employers at Church House, Westminster, in 1967. Designed for 'executives responsible for interviewing undergraduates', it was addressed amongst others by Michael Argyll, an academic psychologist at the University of Oxford who was particularly interested in all forms of communication, including the field of non-verbal communication. His contribution was particularly well received and several companies approached CRAC requesting in-house interview training.

In response, a series of three-day residential courses was designed in consultation with Michael Argyll and Elizabeth Sidney who, with

EDUCATION
Crosland's managers

A novel form of training for teachers took place at Sussex University last week. The Careers Research and Advisory Centre and the Tavistock Institute of Human Relations sponsored a workshop session for about thirty heads on the theme of secondary school administration in the 1970s.

Head teachers are normally in a position of sole authority. But, ironically, on this course there was a reversal to the pupil role: some were worried by not being told what to do. They had, it seems, expected lectures and seminars, but not the rigours of the workshop techniques—designed to allow them to use their own resources more, with some guidance ("input") from workshop staff.

An initial handicap was the sociological jargon. Another, the fundamental doubt that industrial management techniques could be applied to schools. But at the end of the three day session, it was quite clear that many head teachers present (responsible for schools of 2,000 or more) saw themselves as having tasks which were not unlike managers in industry. A success for the famous—and unpopular—Crosland image of the teacher as manager.

The teachers were preoccupied with such issues as how to allocate the time and energy of the head teacher to the management of the non-professional teaching aspects of the school. They began to struggle with the idea of developing a practical and managerial philosophy for schools: how could you delegate responsibility, and yet keep a degree of control for the head? What should be the relationship of the school to the community?

The most helpful "input" was from a member of the Tavistock Institute staff on the change in pattern of traditional industry. Traditionally industry, with the aim of maximising profit, has relied on an organisational structure which depends on coercion, job splitting and close supervision. The new pattern of industrial organisation, it was claimed, aims to maximise industry's contribution to society. In such situations management should see itself as having a service function, aiming to provide job enjoyment for its employees and minimal job specification. Teachers should see that it was far better for them to be able to help create a social environment in which people liked to work, rather than those in which they see the job (school) as occupying only a tiny fragment of their existence.

Reproduced from *New Society,* 20 April 1967.

Margaret Stone, had co-authored the authoritative *The Skills of Interviewing* (published by Tavistock Publications in 1961). These courses, in which actual undergraduates were paid to be interviewed in training sessions for recruiters, evolved into the 'Interview Techniques Training Programme Kit', launched by CRAC in February 1968. The Programme provided trainers with the necessary materials to organise their own course of between three and six days within their own organisation. The Kit included a Trainer's Manual, five films, a tape recording and assorted Notes. Developed for CRAC by Mantra Ltd (a company established by Sidney), it was widely used by companies throughout the country.

Head Teachers as Managers

By the late 1960s there was a wide acceptance that more time needed to be allotted to careers education in schools, for which materials were now far more readily available. At CRAC Boehm held discussions with an associate, Geoffrey Caston (Joint Secretary of the Schools Council and previously Assistant Secretary in the Department of Education), which highlighted the key issue of the attitudes of head teachers. With secondary education in a state of complete re-organisation and smaller schools being merged into much larger comprehensives, staff lacked the strategic management training necessary to meet these new demands. Many heads retained a narrow vision about the role of their schools and often it seemed that a head's principal aim was to focus on achieving successful university admissions figures at the expense of wider questions concerning social education, citizenship and careers. Caston was keen on the idea of a course to address this issue and Boehm took the idea to Professor Tommy Wilson, who had helped with the Graduate Schools and had been a co-founder of the Tavistock Institute of Human Relations in the late 1940s. Wilson suggested the Institute as an ideal partner for the project and a three-day course for head teachers called 'Secondary School Administration for the 1970s' was developed, the first of which was held at Sussex University in 1967. Participating headteachers were personally invited by the Schools Council, which paid their expenses and CRAC's fees.

At the opening session of the course the headteachers were asked to talk about what they believed to be their objectives as heads and what were they hoping to get out of the course. The initial response to such a discussion instead of the usual introductory lecture was frosty. But the ensuing discussion generated key questions about a school's wider responsibilities within its community, about the status of the parental

Some of CRAC's 'media partnerships'

voice in the educational process and about a school's responsibility for the longer-term success of its pupils. This in turn raised questions about adequate resourcing and a fair share of curriculum space for careers education. The course met the Schools Council's aim of 'opening up the careers education debate' and was repeated several times for them by CRAC.

Media Partnerships
CRAC continued to strengthen its press relations and from 1967 several members of staff including Klaus Boehm, Richard Slessor, Veronica Matthew and Clare Bosanquet contributed to a weekly 'CRAC Careers and Education' column for the Saturday *Financial Times*, covering subjects ranging from 'Entering Business Today' to 'Careers in Art' and 'Women, Careers and Marriage' to 'Life with a Computer'. Boehm wrote a further piece for the FT suggesting that university careers advice should be axed, with the money saved redirected towards careers information. Inevitably, the article cause considerable controversy, particularly with disgruntled careers officers.

A year earlier the *Sun* had launched a weekly 'CRAC Careers Column' with a personal careers advice and information service for its readers. The uptake was significant and placed extra pressure on the CRAC Information Service, which by 1967 was dealing with 1,600 questions a year from its own subscribers.

CRAC also provided columns for the *Sunday Telegraph* (a series of articles on 'Careers for School-Leavers' by Boehm) and the *Daily Express*. Bridgewater discussed career choice in a BBC Home Service programme, *Parents and Adolescents*, and appeared on a BBC2 Television programme dealing with full-time courses outside universities. He was also invited to address the Annual Conference of the British Institute of Management.

Watts's Departure and New Projects
The end of 1967 was marked by the temporary departure of Tony Watts. To deepen his research skills and his theoretical understanding of careers issues, he enrolled at the University of York to study for an MPhil in Sociology. His thesis on the nature of the choices students have to make and the impact of those choices was published in 1972 by Routledge & Kegan Paul as *Diversity and Choice in Higher Education*.

Despite the temporary loss of one of its founders, there was no let-up in CRAC's momentum. The St Andrews Street offices had become palpably unsuitable and in March 1968 CRAC moved to Bateman Street,

The main office of the Careers Research and Advisory Centre in Bateman Street, Cambridge, from 1968 to 1980. It was formerly a theological college.

renting 12,000 square feet in the western wing of Cheshunt Building, formerly a theological college, described as 'a delightful piece of Arts and Crafts Gothic'. Its new owners had failed to uncover a covenant in the property's freehold title deeds restricting its use to educational purposes. Bridgewater was therefore able to negotiate a rate 80% lower than the local average rents for equivalent property.

Aware that CRAC could learn much from the USA, Bridgewater had gone there for talks with the USA College Placement Council (the North American equivalent of the Standing Conference of University Appointments Services), the American Management Association and various schools organisations. He was invited to give a presentation at the American Association of Placement Officers' Annual conference at Lehigh University setting out the aims and methodology of the CRAC Undergraduate Schools Programme. In his conclusion he said:

'The CRAC Schools are a unique method of conveying occupational information to undergraduates at a time when many of them have not even thought about their future careers. The contact with the young executives enables many of the undergraduates to measure their own intellectual capabilities against specific industrial career demands. The schools set out to give information to undergraduates and industry's active participation helps bridge the communications gap between industry and the universities. These CRAC Schools are only one part of a process which must be accelerated and enlarged if Britain is to utilise effectively one of its most valuable resources —trained manpower.'

1968 began with a seminar on American recruitment techniques for UK employers confronted by the 'brain drain' of science and engineering graduates to the USA, where funding science and technology was an important Cold War strategy. The 'brain drain' had been on the manpower agenda in earnest since the publication of a report, *Emigration of Scientists from the United Kingdom*, by the Royal Society in 1963. The CRAC event had been devised and set up by Bridgewater during his visit to USA and was led by T.W. Harrington Jr (Director of Placement at Massachussetts Institute of Technology) and M. Jacoby (of the Olin Mathieson Chemical Corporation), two leading American manpower experts.

Breakthrough Publishing Titles
CRAC was fully aware that, just as with O-level choices, the wrong choice of A-levels could jeopardise a fifth former's choice of degree course and career. Based on extensive research CRAC now published *Upper School Choice* which included comprehensive lists of university

Your Choice Beyond a Degree was first published as a paperback by CRAC in 1972. The book evolved into the leading guide to jobs for undergraduates, *Graduate Employment and Training*.

entrance requirements by O-level as well as A-level entry requirements for all professions.

Beyond a Degree, which originated as an Information Bulletin showing the likely careers consequences of particular degree course choices, evolved into a volume edited by Watts with tabulated charts and articles illustrating graduate destinations subject by subject, based on the research of the Universities' Statistics Committee (and later the Central Services Unit). *Beyond a Degree* became an annual publication, later renamed *Graduate Employment and Training (GET)*. By the early 1990s GET was the leader in the graduate recruitment directories league table, providing a unique comprehensive list of all known graduate recruiters with the latest research on career destinations of graduates by degree subject. This directory was supported by advertising as Volume III of the CRAC/CBI *Yearbook*.

Mapping the Careers Sector

A survey at a CRAC conference for 72 careers teachers held in August 1968 revealed just how important CRAC had become for careers advisers. Its results showed that for the majority, a CRAC course was their only training. Twenty-five respondents received no extra pay for their careers work and 21 were given no teaching time allocation. The vast majority had no telephone, interview room or dedicated funds. These findings were backed up by a joint CRAC/National Union of Teachers (NUT) survey the following year, revealing that only 29% of careers teachers were happy with their resources. Yet in 1969 a joint NUT/Daily Express Careers Service survey found that half of the 2,000 parents interviewed thought that careers training was the single most important topic for their child.

Establishing the Institute of Manpower Studies

Smith and Bartholomew (two IMS Council members) wrote in their study, *Manpower Planning in the United Kingdom: An Historical Review*:

'From about 1962 there was an emerging awareness of an alarming degree of overmanning in British industry, while at the same time there was much talk of overfull employment, labour shortages, skills shortages, and of employers indulging in poaching rather than providing for the future through training... It had been suggested during casual talks at the NATO conference in August 1967 [on manpower planning] that there was a need... for a full-time study unit. This idea was discussed elsewhere, and not least in follow-up to the CRAC conference that summer.'

CRAC Scotland

Director: J. L. Brodie

Panel of Advisers

J. O. Blair-Cunynghame, OBE, Chairman, Royal Bank of Scotland

J. W. Burdin, HMI, Scottish Education Department

J. Collins, Sub-Dean of the Faculty of Science, University of Glasgow

T. R. Craig, CBE, TD, formerly Board Member, British Steel Corporation

A. E. Harper, Personnel Director, Nobel's Explosives Ltd

E. Kerr, PhD, Chief Officer, CNAA

D. McDonald, Managing Director, Parsons Peebles Ltd

C. Melville, Director of Education, Roxburgh Education Authority

The Lord Polwarth, TD, formerly Governor, Bank of Scotland

J. Robertson, Chairman and Managing Director, Whatlings Ltd

G. Scott, Director of Management Services, Yarrow (Shipbuilders) Ltd

The Panel of Advisers met in Edinburgh last December under the Chairmanship of Lord Polwarth. Nine of the eleven members were present and Adrian Bridgewater, CRAC's Director, and John Brodie were in attendance. Mr. Brodie reported on the progress that had been made in Scotland and referred in particular to the expansion of activities associated with the schools' programme of work. This had been mainly prompted by the policy to appoint guidance teachers to promoted posts in Scottish secondary schools and a greater number of teachers than ever before had attended CRAC training courses. Mr. Olaf Thornton, who had just retired from the Panel, was thanked for the help and encouragement he had given over the years.

Publications

While CRAC publications such as *Degree Course Guides*, *Your Choice Beyond a Degree*, the *Yearbook Series* and others are helpful in a Scottish context, it has become evident that there is also a need for other text books and reference books to be developed to meet special Scottish requirements. The appointment of guidance teachers has hastened this situation because there is a serious shortage of suitable material for use in conjunction with the work they are now undertaking as part of timetabled programmes of guidance. As a consequence, CRAC Scotland has been working on new publications during the course of the year and some of these are listed below.

Star River Project The copyright of this Project is held by Esso Petroleum Company, and CRAC has been invited to publish it as a result of the Scottish Education Department's decision to develop some simulation material for use in conjunction with the Certificate in Sixth Year Studies which would show the students the economic and social consequences of their academic work. Star River is about the problems associated with developing a ten-year programme for cleaning up a system of Scottish rivers and involves decisions of an economic and social industrial and government nature. While a certain amount of work remains to be done before Star River appears in its final form it is expected that it will be published early in 1973.

Career Decisions This has been written by two well-known Scottish educationalists against a background of knowledge and experience of Scottish education and employment conditions. The manuscript was completed during 1971/72 and has already been submitted to CRAC. It is designed primarily as a classroom text book for pupils in the 13 to 15+ age range, who will probably leave school age 16, and it is structured in such a way that teachers will be able to use it as a basis for a careers programme whether over an extended period or concentrated in a shorter space of time, depending upon timetable constraints. It is not yet available, but will be fully publicised in due course.

Yearbook of Education and Training Opportunities The third Scottish edition of Volume I of the CRAC/CBI Yearbook was published in March 1972. This Scottish edition consists of the British Yearbook with a separate section of Scottish entries. This has now developed to such an extent that it is hoped that it will be possible to publish a completely separate Scottish Yearbook for 1974/75.

Courses

Over 500 teachers, university and college staff, careers officers, employers and others attended CRAC Scotland courses and conferences in 1971/72, and this represented a further increase on the previous year.

Guidance and the Curriculum, Baird Hall of Residence, Glasgow, 20–22 December 1971.

The aim of this course was to illustrate the design of integrated programmes of guidance and involve participants in designing a programme for use in a particular type of school. Course participants were trained in the administration, interpretation and uses of the *Crowley Occupational Interest Blank*, and were shown new materials and aids in the field of careers guidance. One highlight of the course was a talk given by Professor Stanley Cramer of the Department of Counselling, State University of New York at Buffalo. He was in Britain attached to CRAC's Guidance Unit for four months, and at the course he gave an account of the main differences he had been able to identify between British and American practices, which was both informative and entertaining. Professor Cramer believed strongly in the need for full-time counsellors in schools, and he forecast that despite the substantial body of opinion in Scotland which opposed this view it was inevitable that such a policy would have to be adopted ultimately.

Chairman: J. R. Calderwood, Lecturer, Dundee College of Education and P. B. Bell, Assistant Headmaster, Grange Secondary School, Glasgow.

Attendance: 100.

Admission to Higher Education in Scotland, Baird Hall of Residence, Glasgow 28–30 March 1972.

This course was designed to give admissions staff from

In 1968 the Ministry of Labour's Manpower Research Unit was under heavy criticism. An effective forecasting body was in widespread demand from government, employers, economists and a few sophisticated careers advisers. Colin Leicester's contribution on the subject in the CRAC *Journal* in 1964 had attracted favourable attention. The Ministry of Defence had very large manpower requirements and was particularly unhappy that there was no reliable forecasting mechanism. In 1967 Boehm had discussed the question of establishing a dedicated manpower research base. This encouraged Boehm and Bridgewater to initiate high-level talks involving the Ministry of Defence on how such a research base might perhaps be financed and realised by establishing a CRAC satellite.

Headed by Sir Peter Allen, Chairman of ICI, and co-ordinated for CRAC by Boehm, a major fundraising campaign was launched and sufficient backing was obtained quite quickly. In 1968 the new Institute of Manpower Studies (IMS) was set up within the University of Sussex, with an independent governing body of its own and strong representation from CRAC. Bridgewater, Boehm and Parry Rogers, a member of CRAC's Council, were appointed to the founding Council. Boehm later resigned from CRAC to become its full-time Secretary.

Under its first President, Lord Jackson, the IMS's first five years of activity were underwritten by a group of some twenty companies and what was then the Civil Service Department. Subsequently, it became self-financing, undertaking apolitical research and consultancy and disseminating its findings. The IMS continued to wield significant influence with the Heath government, which had been elected against a backdrop of relative economic health and which was keen to harness the education system to the country's economic needs.

Renamed the Institute of Employment Studies, IMS celebrated its 40th year in 2008. The establishment of the IMS illustrated how CRAC could grasp a needs-based opportunity and develop it to take root in an environment other than its own Cambridge base.

A New Director for Scotland
In 1968, Bridgewater asked the Director of the CBI's Scottish Office for help in CRAC's search for a new Director for Scotland. He recommended the Education Secretary of CBI Scotland, John Brodie, who was duly appointed. The Scottish education system already had a structure of guidance teachers (both educational and personal), many of whom were very inexperienced, and Brodie was aware of this ready market for courses and materials. Whilst many of CRAC's Scottish

Advice on careers

The first national careers exhibition was opened on Tuesday at the Empire Hall, Olympia. Opportunity 70, which is sponsored by the *Daily Express,* includes 177 exhibitors from a wide variety of trades, professions and education and is designed to give advice and information to school-leavers and careers teachers. It will run until December 15 and is free to schoolchildren and those accompanying them.

Mrs. Margaret Thatcher, Secretary of State for Education, when she opened the exhibition said that there would be wider opportunities open to school leavers in the 1970s in further and higher education but some of the facilities would be wasted unless parents and pupils knew what was on offer, where to obtain advice and how to get on the appropriate course and what grants are available.

About 50,000 schoolchildren are expected to visit Olympia. Staff of the Careers Research Advisory Council (C.R.A.C.) and the ornmarket Careers Centre are on hand to give advice at the routing and information centre in the main lobby.

Margaret Thatcher, Secretary of State for Education and Science, opening the National Careers Exhibition, Olympia, in December 1970.

operations were fundamentally the same as those administered from Cambridge, Brodie set up his own Advisory Committee (with considerable help from Lord Polwarth, then chairman of the Scottish Council for Development and Industry) to liaise closely with all parts of the Scottish system. The Scottish courses were soon over-subscribed and Brodie managed to secure sponsorship from local businesses to supplement funding provided by CRAC in Cambridge.

In May 1970 the CRAC Scottish Office ran its first 'Post-Graduate School', and by 1973 over 500 people were participating annually in CRAC Scotland courses and conferences. Its other activities included a new termly magazine, *Guidance Scotland*. CRAC's contribution to the development of guidance in Scotland was acknowledged by the Scottish Education Department, Brodie recalling "the tremendous amount of encouragement" that it offered him for CRAC's activities.

A National Careers Exhibition
In December of 1970 the first National Careers Exhibition was held at London Olympia and CRAC was commissioned to develop and provide material for all visiting school groups and to create a unique routing system for groups to navigate more easily around the Exhibition. To get this job Bridgewater negotiated with the then President of the National Union of Students, Jack Straw, future British Home Secretary, Foreign Secretary and Minister of State for Justice. The Exhibition was opened by Margaret Thatcher as Education Minister and she was seen going around the Show with a large folder under her arm presented to her by Bridgewater emblazoned with the words 'What is CRAC?'

Securing the Finances
The review of the organisation's financial situation at the turn of the new decade was less than satisfactory. Donations to the Foundation Fund, mainly in the form of seven-year covenants, were providing around £3,000 per annum, a useful injection but inadequate to cover the operating cost shortfalls. Despite early optimism CRAC had been returning operating losses and in February 1969 the CRAC Council had initiated a financial viability study. Peter Spanoghe, a former teacher who had recently joined the CRAC Council and was an executive director of Rio Tinto Zinc (RTZ), suggested that if a clear plan were put to RTZ their Board might be persuaded to make a short-term loan. Bridgewater presented his dilemma and his proposals for the future at a breakfast meeting of the full Board of RTZ on 8 November 1969. The meeting agreed that a management consultant from RTZ, Robin Ramm,

CRAC Research and Development Unit

Head of Unit: *A.G. Watts, MA, MPhil*

The Research and Development Unit's staff during the year consisted of the head of the unit, a secretary, and a part-time information assistant; in addition, Professor Paul Lohnes of the State University of New York at Buffalo, a leading vocational development theorist in the USA, was attached to the unit for six months during his sabbatical semester, though most of his time was spent on his own research. The resources of the unit were severely stretched during the year, and it is hoped that the new National Institute for Careers Education and Counselling – into which the unit is to be merged as from 1 January 1975 – will make it possible to expand its work.

The main work of the unit in 1973/74 fell into five areas:

1 Planning of the new Institute
A great deal of the unit's time has been taken up with planning and public relations work for the new Institute. Tony Watts has been a member of the Planning Board which CRAC and The Hatfield Polytechnic set up to prepare plans for the Institute, and has acted as its secretary. He was also on the Hatfield appointments board for the Senior Fellow (Education and Training) who is to be the Polytechnic's first substantive contribution to the Institute; he and Adrian Bridgewater prepared the proposals leading to the Leverhulme Trust's grant; and along with Adrian Bridgewater he conducted the negotiations with Donald Super which led to his acceptance of CRAC's invitation to join the Institute as its Honorary Director and Senior Fellow (Research).

2 Development work
Three major development projects were carried out by the unit during the year. First, it has adapted – in conjunction with David Elsom (a Hertfordshire careers teacher) – some exciting and innovative curriculum materials on decision-making which were initially developed in the USA. These materials have been completely rewritten for UK use and were field-tested in twelve schools and two colleges of further education in the autumn term of 1973. They have now been published under the title *Deciding*.

Second, the unit has developed some curriculum materials on sex-roles, designed to help secondary-school pupils to question their attitudes to sex-roles in the home and at work, and to show them the variety of alternative patterns that are possible. This project was conducted in conjunction with Anne Jones (a teacher) and Jan Marsh (a journalist), and the materials were field-tested in thirteen schools in the spring term of 1974. They are to be published towards the end of 1974 under the title *Male and Female*, which it is hoped will be the first of a new CRAC Life-Style Series.

Third, Tony Watts was commissioned by IBM (UK) Limited in July 1974 to review the Interactive Careers Guidance System which IBM have developed in conjunction with the Cheshire County Council. He spent a week in the two schools operating the system, and his 46-page report is to be published by the IBM Scientific Centre.

3 Training
The unit was responsible for planning and co-ordinating six of the residential courses and seven of the one-day courses described on pages 4-5, and also for administering the CRAC course modules (see page 3). In addition, Tony Watts directed a three-day course on *Vocational Counselling in the Open University* for 53 Regional Directors, Senior Counsellors and other staff of the Open University, which was held at Woburn on 18-20 February; and he organised and chaired a consultation on *Counselling in Work Settings* which was organised by CRAC in conjunction with the Standing Conference for the Advancement of Counselling and was held at Rugby on 4-6 June 1974. These two projects were opened up the area of non-career counselling as a possible new area of activity both for CRAC and for the new Institute. Tony Watts also delivered 12 lectures to outside groups during the year (see below).

4 Dissemination of research
The unit has not yet engaged in any basic research: this is being left until the Institute is established. It has however made a major effort to disseminate the results of research work being done elsewhere both to other research workers and also to guidance practitioners. During 1973/74 it has done this in four main ways:

- Through the *British Journal of Guidance and Counselling*, which is published by CRAC and of which Tony Watts is an editor. This journal is now widely recognised as the leading British journal in the guidance field, and has also built up a considerable number of overseas subscriptions.

- Through an abstracting service which involves over twenty academics and guidance practitioners and is co-ordinated by the unit. The service covers all of the major journals in the field, and is incorporated in the *British Journal of Guidance and Counselling*.

- Through the *Register of Research in Educational and Vocational Guidance* which is run in conjunction with the National Foundation for Educational Research and is maintained by the unit. There are plans to make this register more widely available.

- Through the research seminar described on page 5.

5 Outside commitments
One of the most important functions of the unit has been to associate CRAC's work more closely with that of other bodies working in the guidance field. In addition to the projects mentioned above, Tony Watts during 1973/74 has sat on the Executive Committees of the Standing Conference for the Advancement of Counselling and the International Round Table for the Advancement of Counselling. IRTAC's 1974 conference – attracting over 400 delegates from all over the world – was held in Cambridge, and the unit helped in planning the conference. Tony Watts was also invited to join a Sub-Committee on Training set up by the Association for Student Counselling, an Ad Hoc Group for the Review of Personnel Selection Testing, and a Working Party on the Provision of an Occupational Data Bank set up by the Department of Employment; and he represented CRAC on the Consultative Committee of the Schools Council Careers Education and Guidance Project.

Reproduced from CRAC Annual Report 1973/74.

would review financial management systems and that RTZ would immediately provide a two-year loan of £25,000. The loan was fully repaid in 16 months.

Ramm installed new systems of cost allocation, accounting and budgetary control, and a clear picture of the true cost of each service soon emerged. Whereas 70% of CRAC's income each year was earned from publishing which generated surpluses, the remaining 30%, comprising Teacher Training Services and Student Programmes, was losing money. The financial problem for CRAC was that the surpluses from publications were constantly used up to provide working capital to meet their design, print and distribution costs. Hence CRAC's need for working capital. With this clear distinction between the Publications and Training Services came the first intimation that CRAC would almost certainly need fundamental restructuring.

A new Membership Subscription Scheme was put in place which allowed employers to make a single annual donation scaled to match their interest in CRAC's non-profit-making programmes – usually under deed of covenant. A revision of the Memorandum and Articles of Association allowed for this new Membership Scheme with its wider membership drawn from institutions and organisations supporting CRAC's work.

The Research and Development Unit

Tony Watts, having achieved his postgraduate degree, now returned to CRAC in 1970 to run a new Research and Development Unit with one assistant. It had always been Watts's intention to return to CRAC, which he believed offered greater opportunity '*to change things*' than a conventional academic post. The initial aim of the unit was:

'*... to evaluate and develop existing CRAC publications and services... to identify new areas of need in the light of educational and employment changes, and to develop new publications, courses and other services to meet the changing patterns.*'

Watts had met, among many others, Dr Peter Daws, Director of the Vocational Guidance Research Unit at the University of Leeds, who later became Senior Lecturer in Education at the University of Keele. Daws asked CRAC to publish his new book, *A Good Start in Life*, which provided an analysis of modern theory and techniques in vocational guidance. The book looked at careers guidance in terms beyond a narrow psychometric approach, linking it into broader ideas of counselling and mental health. This publication strengthened CRAC's credentials as a publisher of theoretical as well as practical works.

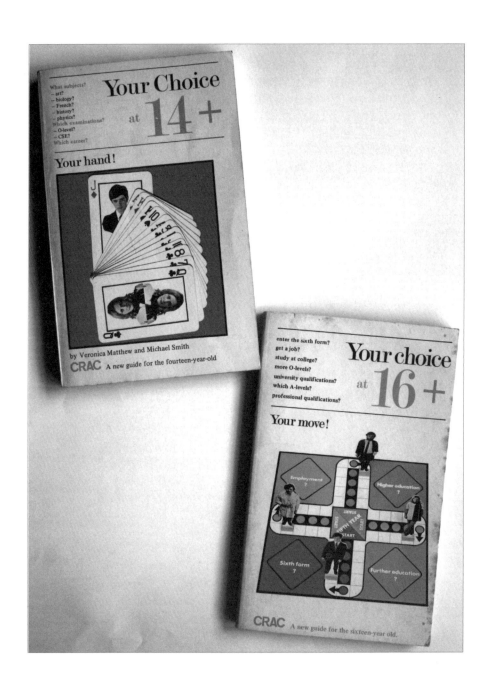

Two of CRAC's most successful publications, first published in paperback in 1972.

With the increase in classroom-based careers education, the schools needed new materials and CRAC editors worked with the Research and Development Unit to produce the *Bull's Eye* series that was launched in 1972. Written in simple language by Tony Crowley, a careers adviser in Hertfordshire, it was eye-catchingly illustrated in full colour by Althea Braithwaite, a well-known author and illustrator of children's books including her *Dinosaur Series*. The first three titles, *Choosing a Job*, *Finding a Job* and *Starting a Job*, were an immediate sales success, selling over 20,000 copies of each title in their first year. The *Guardian* reprinted pages from the series alongside enthusiastic reviews.

By 1973 the CRAC Research and Development Unit was at the forefront of developing curriculum and teaching materials, as well as an underpinning theoretical rationale, in response to what the CRAC *Annual Report* described as:

'*The increasing awareness of schools that careers education is a subject which can justly demand time in the curriculum.*'

Although time allotted to the subject was prone to significant regional differences, about a quarter of UK schools were now allowing careers teachers to spend at least one-fifth of their time exclusively on careers education, and CRAC with its Research and Development Unit developed a series of classroom books and other teaching materials to support these developments. For example, *Decide for Yourself,* by Dr Bill Law of the University of Reading, helped fifth and sixth formers to understand their own interests, abilities, needs, values and personality more fully.

The Robbins-inspired rise in the number of university applicants had inevitably caused an upsurge in the number of students who failed to obtain a place on their favoured course or at their desired institution. In the early 1970s CRAC was the first to respond to this new need by publishing *Rethink*, an annual guide for school leavers confronting such a situation and reconsidering their post-school plans.

In 1972, Watts was awarded a Travel Fellowship by the US State Department under its Leaders and Specialists Programme to undertake a one-month study visit to the USA. In the course of this visit, he met most of the leading thinkers and developers in the careers field, and studied the new computer-aided career guidance systems that were just beginning to emerge. On his return, the Unit worked with IBM to develop and evaluate the first major system of this kind in the UK.

Another innovative idea brought back from America by Watts – following a lead from Bridgewater's earlier visits – was the *Deciding* programme. It taught pupils how to make decisions on topics including

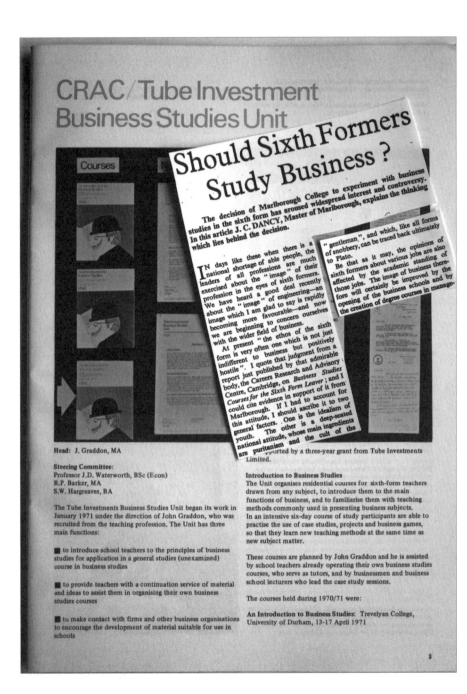

CRAC's Business Studies Unit as described in the 1970/71 Director's Report.

'lifestyle' issues, with investigations into the relationships between work, leisure and community. Working with a teacher, David Elsom, Watts adapted the American materials to develop and field-test CRAC's own *Deciding* programme, a classroom book with separate *Notes* for pupils and teachers.

In 1973 Bridgewater was invited to join the Government Working Party on Technological Aids to Guidance. He was also on the selection panel for the post of Director of the newly created Schools Council Project on Careers Education and Guidance, to be based in Cambridge, which would later offer many opportunities for co-operation and collaboration.

Also in 1973, CRAC launched the *British Journal of Guidance and Counselling*, co-edited by Tony Watts with a distinguished Editorial Advisory Board and described as '... *the first British academic/professional journal in the guidance and counselling field*'.

A Dedicated Business Studies Unit

Business Studies had become established in school curricula since the mid-1960s (both within General Studies and as an A-level subject in its own right), and CRAC had created a separate specialist department to service and develop this new field. Bridgewater believed that this department could be turned into a distinct Unit which might be able to expand faster business sponsorship. He had strong contacts with the Board of the international engineering firm, Tube Investments, and in 1971 he was able to persuade its Board to sponsor a new TI/CRAC Business Education Unit, the stated aims of which were:

1) To promote a better overall understanding by sixth formers of the business world.

2) To assist careers and subject teachers in stimulating the interests of their students in careers in business.

3) To encourage liaison between schools and firms.

The Unit, which operated with its own staff under John Graddon, a former grammar-school economics teacher, developed classroom materials including case studies and business games and ran residential courses to train teachers how to use them in Business Studies, Economics, General Studies and Careers lessons. Additionally, it compiled a register of companies, employees, regional CBI offices and Chambers of Commerce willing to provide support to local schools. Over 1,000 teachers used the Unit's products and services in five years.

Improved Business Systems

Evidence that the new financial control systems were beginning to get results began to emerge:

'... *whereas publications earned a small surplus, the Schools Programme recorded substantial losses, which was almost exactly made up by the contributions of Members.*'

The organisation supplied over half a million books, booklets and other teaching materials in 1973. These included over 50,000 sales of *Your Choice at 14+*, the successor to *Middle School Choice*.

The acquisition of *Graduate Studies* in March 1973, a directory of postgraduate academic opportunities, completed the CRAC range of factual information on all UK educational qualifications from secondary school to postgraduate and professional courses.

CRAC was no longer a small voice in a scarcely developed sector but had become an established and influential voice in the much matured (though still evolving) careers education field. As far back as 1969, *Technical Education* had published an article arguing that whilst '*CRAC is not exactly a pressure group...it can claim some indirect credit for a general change of attitude over careers*'.

With its growing portfolio and increasing financial turnover, CRAC now needed to review its organisational structure and assess how it could best continue to fulfill its original aims.

6
Changing Needs: New Solutions

By its tenth anniversary in 1974, CRAC was operating in a much-changed careers environment. The maturation of the sector was punctuated by a series of official reports and legislative advances that had made careers education and guidance a key theme in the national educational debate. Furthermore, the sector was now populated by numerous new bodies that were well-organised and communicative, a situation very different from 1964 when practitioners had tended to work independently, resulting in a largely fractured and unco-ordinated careers advice infrastructure.

The Continuing Impact of Robbins
The beginnings of CRAC in 1964 had, as outlined in Chapter 1, coincided with the appearance of the Robbins Report, the impact of which was still being realised in the 1970s. Robbins had demanded the rapid expansion of the higher education system so that courses might be 'available for all those who are qualified by ability and attainment to pursue them and who wish to do so'. This, the report argued, was essential because:

'Both in general cultural standards and in competitive intellectual power, vigorous action is needed to avert the danger of a serious relative decline in this country's standing.'

The Conservative government of Sir Alec Douglas-Home had responded to the report's publication by setting out a ten-year expansion plan with a budget of some £3.5 million. From the 1960s to 1974 the number of students taking first degrees was up from 92,000 to 217,000, studying either at universities or, from 1965, at polytechnics. Thirty such institutions were established between 1965 and 1973 under the direction of the Secretary for Education, Anthony Crosland. Controlled by local authorities, the polytechnics specialised in vocational courses but were not allowed to award their own degrees, offering those of the Council for National Academic Awards instead. Cheaper to run than universities, they allowed for a steep increase in student numbers and later, under Conservative legislation in the 1990s, would become universities each with their own charter.

The relevance of the Robbins expansion to careers education and guidance was clear:

'... *we deceive ourselves if we claim that more than a small fraction of students in institutions of higher education would be where they are if there were no significance for their future careers.*'

Following an unprecedented increase in the number of higher education institutions, student numbers and courses available, the higher education sector of the mid-70s bore only a vague resemblance to that of the mid-60s. As we have seen, much of CRAC's early work was undertaken as a direct response to the Robbins Report's demand for more and better information for potential undergraduates, their teachers and families who were unaware of '*the wide range of courses available in universities and elsewhere*'. The report went on to emphasise that:

'*...the links between university institutions and government research establishments and industry should be strengthened...*'

While CRAC had made massive strides in tackling these issues, there remained vast amounts to do. With student numbers continuing to grow during the 1970s and beyond, the amount and complexity of information that needed to be communicated between the institutions, students, schools and employers was continuing to grow too.

Modernising the University Appointments Boards and the Graduate Recruiters

This fundamental overhaul of higher education also brought about a restructuring of the university appointments services, the traditional front-line sources of careers information and advice for university students. As early as 1955 the universities had combined to establish a Statistics Committee responsible for assembling and disseminating information on subjects such as graduate career destinations. However, beyond this there was little formal co-operation between services until the foundation of the Standing Committee of University Appointments Services (SCUAS) in 1967. The importance of the services was accepted by the 1964 Heyworth Report, which acknowledged that the university appointments boards had a valid '*claim to a fair share of available funds*'. It also recommended that the advisory provision of the services be strengthened and the establishment of a central services unit be considered to carry out certain functions, such as keeping a register of employers.

Bill Kirkman, one of the driving forces behind establishment of SCUAS and its president from 1971 to 1973, recalled that by the time of a 1965 conference of university appointments officers in Edinburgh:

'There was growing recognition of the case for something more formal than ad hoc *collaboration between services.'*

With a greater number of graduates moving into more and broader areas of the labour market than ever before, the traditional UAB structure was coming under increasing strain. As a result a committee was instituted to investigate the possibility of establishing a more formal umbrella organisation. Two years later SCUAS (later renamed the Association of Graduate Careers Advisory Services (AGCAS)) was founded to facilitate better communication, to pool knowledge and to co-ordinate efforts at a national level. Chaired by Neil Scott of Nottingham University, its early initiatives included the administration of a graduate vacancies 'Clearing House', based at the University of Manchester, which sought to match unfilled positions with suitable candidates. With the agreement of the Committee of Vice-Chancellors and Principals, this project led to the creation of the Central Services Unit (CSU; now Graduate Prospects), a service of the type Heyworth had recommended. The CSU kept a register of employers and graduates, researched and distributed statistical information on subjects including salaries and employment patterns, and took over the work of the Clearing House in 1972, in which year it included details of 14,500 vacancies from 2,500 employers.

SCUAS also played an influential role in the formation of the Standing Conference of Employers of Graduates (SCOEG), as the universities realised the need for better channels of communication with those responsible for graduate recruitment. Bridgewater recalled a rather secretive discussion led by Martin Higham of Rowntrees at CRAC's 1968 Winter Conference for Employers at Magdalene College, Cambridge, about the need for a new employers' group. This and CRAC's other conferences provided further impetus for the idea.

SCOEG came into being at the SCUAS conference in Durham in 1969 as an independent, not-for-profit organisation bringing together the experience of graduate recruiters throughout the country. It aimed to serve as a forum for discussion on recruitment policy, to facilitate contact with university and other appontments boards, to disseminate information about methods of recruitment and graduate qualifications, and to assist in improving recruitment and selection techniques. Although early membership came mainly from the industrial sector, it quickly expanded to include representatives from a disparate range of professions, including banking, accountancy, law, the armed services and the Civil Service. In 1987 SCOEG was renamed the Association of Graduate Recruiters (AGR).

A Shortage of Scientists

A number of reports in the latter part of the 1960s highlighted the continuing shortfall in the number of scientists, technologists and engineers required to meet the national need, despite Robbins's call for:

'... a growth in the proportion of students taking science and, particularly, technology...'

This plea for closer ties between educational institutions and employers was reiterated in the 1968 Swann Report on *The Flow into Employment of Scientists, Engineers and Technologists*, set up to establish a course of action to address the shortage of science and engineering graduates going into non-academic work or into school teaching.

A related 1968 enquiry into the flow of candidates in science and technology into higher education was led by Lord Dainton. Dainton noted that:

'*In its report of January 1965, the Universities' Central Council on Admissions reported that in pure science universities would have admitted 1,080 more students if suitable candidates had presented themselves, and they also could have admitted 420 more students in technology.*'

Dainton drew special attention to the lack of graduate teachers of mathematics and advised that provision be made for school pupils of all ages and abilities to receive broader and higher-quality maths and science teaching. In addition, the report recommended an incentive scheme to attract more good-quality science and maths graduates into the teaching profession.

Swann and Dainton were followed by the 1969 Haslegrave Report, commissioned by the National Advisory Council on Education for Industry and Commerce '*to review the provision for courses suitable for technicians at all levels...and to consider what changes are desirable in the present structure of courses and examinations*'. It concluded that the existing pattern of exams and courses was not suitable for meeting either the current requirements of industry or those expected to arise in the future. To remedy the situation it suggested the formation of a Technician Education Council and a Business Education Council to oversee planning and co-ordination of courses. Between them, Swann, Dainton and Haslegrave illustrated the necessity for employers and educationalists to communicate so that students might be taught a suitable curriculum to the required standard, and also so that they might be made aware of the real-life relevance of their studies and of the career opportunities presented by following particular academic paths. This was a philosophy central to CRAC's activities.

The Schools System

The radical changes in careers provision in schools were no less significant than those in higher education in the decade to 1974, with careers education becoming prominent in the curriculum, greater recognition of the particular skills needed to provide careers advice and guidance, and the emergence of a Careers Service to replace the Youth Employment Service. A series of reports had set the scene for change.

The recommendation of the Crowther and Newsom reports that the school leaving age be raised from 15 to 16 finally became law in 1972. This provided more time for rounded careers advice to those leaving school at 16, and for responding to Newsom's appeal for more structured activities to prepare school leavers for what lay beyond the classroom walls.

Around the same time, much of what both Albemarle and Evenden called for (see Chapter 2) was implemented when the Careers Service was established in 1973 in succession to the YES.

Commenting on the late 1960s and into the mid-1970s, Peter Daws wrote that:

'*...awareness of the educational, social and economic value of career guidance had continued to grow throughout the period.*'

In the years 1965–70, Anthony Crosland, Secretary of State for Education in the Wilson administration, oversaw the rapid expansion of the comprehensive sector, with larger schools catering for a student body covering the whole ability range. Despite the attempts of Margaret Thatcher, Education Minister under Edward Heath from 1970 to 1974, to stall the trend, the majority of LEAs had abandoned the selective school system by 1975 and careers education was increasingly finding a place on the timetable. According to Bill Law:

'*By the early 1970s, government policies... were beginning to specify coverage for careers education and guidance...*'

The increased school sizes, mixture of abilities and the rise in the leaving age to sixteen accentuated the need for a careers education policy that could be adapted for all pupils. In 1969 E. Rodknight's 'A Survey of Careers Work in Schools' (published in the CRAC *Journal)* reported that half of schools had 'careers' as a timetabled subject for final-year leavers. A few years later, the Department of Education and Science's 1973 report, *Careers Education in Secondary Schools*, found that two-thirds of schools offered careers education (with provision in secondary moderns and comprehensives far higher than in grammar schools). In 1974 Nicola Cherry's study, 'Do Careers Officers Give Good Advice?' (published in CRAC's new academic journal), provided empirical evidence of the value of careers advice in a study of the early careers of 5,362 young people. Cherry wrote:

'90% of the 15-year-old school leavers in the sample were recommended by the Youth Employment Service to take up a particular sort of work. Survey members who followed this advice stayed longer in their first job than young people who took up some other work. Evidence is presented which suggests that this improved performance results... from the accurate assessment by the careers officer of their abilities and interests.'

The growth of the comprehensive schools sector allowed for some radical innovation, no better epitomised than by the Stantonbury Campus School in Milton Keynes. The largest comprehensive school in the country, it opened in 1974 under the direction of Geoff Cooksey, who had been Joint Secretary of the Schools Council from 1967-72. Cooksey described Stantonbury as an *'environment in which the individual can enjoy and extend himself through the fullest use of the resources which only a large community can offer'*.

Cooksey's association with CRAC had begun several years earlier when he was the headmaster of Shirebrook Secondary School in Mansfield and oversaw a conference for them (the first of many) in Nottingham in 1967. Cooksey recalled of that period:

'Up to the beginning of the 1960s careers education didn't figure in any real sense in the schools curriculum... Secondary modern schools had more sense of it as their students were more locally tied to the community. There were lots of examples of them doing good work with local industry. They should receive some credit for relating their work to the needs of the children when they left school... Then comprehensive schools came in recognising their responsibility to all their pupils and their community. There was a movement to making education more relevant for most of their pupils. And that was a seed bed in which careers education could begin to grow... At Shirebrook we introduced careers education as an intrinsic part of the weekly curriculum, run largely through a tutorial system and based primarily on having a careers department. It was a mining area with high unemployment. We wanted to broaden the occupational opportunities available to the children.'

Of Stantonbury he said:

'All the barriers were down. You could do at Milton Keynes what you wouldn't dare to do in the heart of London or Birmingham... We believed that careers education was fundamentally at the heart of the whole education system and we were part of what I see as the shift away from

the liberal education at the beginning of the twentieth century to the more broadly functional education that you got at the end of it. What you're going to do with your education is more important than the fact that you acquired a liberal background.'

Among many innovations, the school curriculum was suspended for one day each fortnight when pupils were sent on a range of fieldwork projects, including visits to local businesses. Children were also assigned tutors for two or three years at a time to monitor educational progress and career aspirations. Staff and pupils were regularly sent on CRAC courses and the school also built links with local industrial contacts introduced by CRAC.

The Schools Council Careers Project

The Lockwood Report had led to the establishment of the Schools Council in 1964 to disseminate ideas about curricular reform in England and Wales. In 1970 it became an independent body funded equally by the government and local education authorities and played a crucial role in developing careers teaching materials and moving the subject on to the schools curriculum agenda.

As discussed in Chapters 4 and 5, CRAC established close ties with the Council, particularly after the establishment of the CRAC Research and Development Unit. In the mid-1970s Watts was on the steering committee of the Council's Careers Project, which was charged with producing suitable careers education teaching materials for 13- to 18-year-olds, as well as considering broader questions of pedagogy and teacher training. The project was a strong influence on the perception and practice of careers teaching in schools throughout the decade, not least because, as Watts reported, *'the definition of careers education re-emerged as a constant source of debate'*.

The provision of high-quality teaching materials did much to ease the acceptance of the subject on to school curricula, particularly when partnered with innovative approaches to education. Whilst Joint Secretary of the Schools Council, Geoff Cooksey had proposed the Careers Project, of which he said:

'It was a big project that went on for several years. It got through reasonably easily simply because I got CRAC's support for it and their reputation was so high. There was always a good feel about CRAC and everybody I knew admired it.'

Cooksey worked in conjunction with CRAC to produce new services, both when he was on the Schools Council and when he later moved to Stantonbury. One such project was the Personal and Educational

Guidance Simulation (PEGS) board game for teachers to work through the decision-making process necessary to plan a secondary school careers curriculum. As he later commented, PEGS helped teachers '*pin down just what your philosophy was as well as producing the actual working schedule for your school*'.

Nonetheless, despite its increasingly important position within the curriculum, it was not until 1998 that schools were given a statutory duty to provide careers education, and then only to pupils in Years 9, 10 and 11.

The Growth of Careers Education and Counselling

The vocabulary and underpinning theory of the careers sector was going through its own evolution during the late 1960s and early 1970s, with a gradual move from careers advice and guidance towards careers education and counselling. As Watts later wrote in *Rethinking Careers Education and Guidance*:

'*Counselling was concerned with facilitating the process of decision-making, and helping students to take responsibility for the decisions that emerged, rather than being passively dependent on the advice of experts. Counselling on its own could however be a very lengthy and hence expensive way of achieving this goal. For students to make decisions, they needed a conceptual vocabulary, a range of experiences, and a set of decision-making skills, to draw upon. Developmental theories of careeers suggested that such concepts, experiences and skills developed to some extent in the normal process of social maturation. Careers education was based on the premise that such development could be facilitated and, perhaps, accelerated by programmes of deliberate intervention, designed on a group basis.*'

The move towards this more rounded approach could trace its roots back to the work in the 1950s and early 1960s of American academics such as Carl Rogers and Donald Super and British specialists including Peter Daws and Audrey Newsome. In 1963 Keele became the first university to set up an appointments *and counselling* service, with Newsome as its director.

In the 1970s Watts and the CRAC Research and Development Unit were important influences on the development both of careers education and of counselling (including the publication of the *British Journal of Guidance and Counselling*). Other important voices included the CRAC authors Bill Law and Peter Daws. The latter, according to Law:

'*... urged an alternative "comprehensive-matching" model, which* *could accommodate motivations and feelings as well as abilities and aptitudes, but would require more sustained and more skilful help to be offered to students.'*

Professional Teachers' Associations

The nation's careers teachers came under the wing of the National Association of Careers Teachers (later the National Association of Careers and Guidance Teachers, and now the Association for Careers Education and Guidance), which was established at Fitzwilliam College, Cambridge, in 1969, at an ACE-sponsored conference. Its origin was a letter published in the CRAC *Journal* in 1968 by R.P. Heppell of the Grammar Technical School for Boys in South Shields, arguing the need for such an Association (Heppell later became its Secretary and eventually its President); CRAC played a supportive role in getting it off the ground. As the professional association for those providing careers education and guidance to young people, it advocated a belief that the careers officer and the teacher should have a complementary relationship within schools. It also sought to manage the influx of information emanating from the CYEE, publishers, employers and professional associations, and did much to promote in-service training.

By the late 1960s the majority of independent schools had also appointed dedicated careers staff. As David Peck later observed, the Public Schools Appointments Bureau, *'which had seemed to be so threatened by the new Youth Employment Service in the 1950s, began to transform itself'*. Membership was opened up to girls' schools and schools outside the traditional Headmasters' Conference pool and the organisation invested heavily in the use of test-based guidance. In 1970 it restructured itself to become the Independent Schools Careers Organisation (ISCO), an identity retained until it was renamed the Inspiring Futures Foundation in 2007.

The growing status of careers education was illustrated in 1968 by Catherine Avent's appointment as the first careers education adviser of the Inner London Education Authority, and indeed of any LEA in the country. Avent would later write for CRAC, publishing the influential *Practical Approaches to Careers Education* in 1974. At the end of 1970, the first National Careers Exhibition, *Opportunity 70*, was held, with over 250 organisations represented and over 70,000 young people coming through the door. It was another symbol of the increased recognition of the importance of the careers field.

The Employment and Training Act

In preparation for the 1970 general election the Conservative leader, Ted Heath, set up a number of Policy Groups in 1968 and invited Bridgewater, in a private capacity, to join his Education Group. Its Report, *Transition from School to Employment*, drew heavily on Dainton's 1968 Report, *The Flow of Candidates in Science and Technology*, which said that:

'*Subject choices made at school at fourteen and fifteen, are at the moment moving in a direction which will widen the gap between supply and demand for scientists and engineers, for example*'.

The Group stressed the need for the fast development of closer understanding and collabortion between schools, colleges and universities on the one hand and employers on the other. It advised that the Careers Advisory Service should be developed as a national scheme to provide information about courses of further education for the older leaver, but based in the Department of Education and Science rather than the Ministry of Labour.

Heath's Conservative government came to power in June 1970 and its most significant contribution to the sector was the Employment and Training Act of 1973, which aimed to provide '*a satisfactory transition from education to work*' and '*to ensure provision of careers services for school and college students*'. Its main action was, as already noted, to replace the existing YES with a new Careers Service, which was run by the LEAs and staffed by trained careers officers. The Service was obliged to provide guidance for anyone who wanted it up to the age of 18 or until one year after cessation of full-time employment (whichever was later), whilst the pressure applied for an all-age service had resulted in provision for older people on a discretionary basis only.

The Act also provided for the formation in January 1974 of the Manpower Services Commission (MSC), a non-departmental public body of the Department of Employment. Headed by a commission of ten-members chosen from industry, the unions, local authorities and the education sector, the MSC was charged with co-ordinating employment and training services, including Occupational Guidance Units, throughout the UK. The Occupational Guidance Service had been set up in 1966 under the remit of the Department of Employment to provide careers advice to people of all ages (not just the young who were catered for by the Careers Service). However, the service was operated by civil servants with limited in-house training rather than specialist careers advisors, leaving it open to accusations of being more interested in job placement than providing a rounded programme of guidance.

The Open University

The post-Robbins desire to expand access to higher education was in part met by the opening of the Open University to students in 1971. It was the only university to be established in the UK in the ten years following Crosland's implementation of the polytechnic programme in 1965. Individuals who might never have previously considered higher study—whether because of personal circumstances, their age or geographical location—now had the opportunity to 'study at a distance' for a degree. Although its fees were not grant-aided on a mandatory basis, the OU was particularly relevant to those from lower income groups, whose exclusion had been highlighted in 1963 by a Labour Party study group into higher education access, headed by Lord Taylor.

The idea of a 'wireless university' administered in association with the BBC had been mooted since the 1920s, but the rapid developments in communications technology in the 1960s gave renewed momentum to the idea of a non-campus-based university. In 1962 Michael Young wrote an article for *Where?*, proposing an Open University awarding London University degrees. The 1963 Taylor Report then set out its ideas for a 'University of the Air', providing high-quality higher education services via radio and television, an idea that was already being discussed by the BBC and the Ministry of Education.

At the beginning of Harold Wilson's prime ministerial tenure in 1964, he appointed Jennie Lee to develop the 'University of the Air' project, although at this time it was envisaged that existing institutions would pool their resources to produce suitable teaching materials rather than that an entirely new degree-awarding body would be set up. Lee established an advisory committee which submitted a White Paper in 1966 recommending just such a body. After Wilson's re-election in 1967, a Planning Committee was put in place to devise a comprehensive plan for the Open University.

Walter Perry, a Professor of Pharmacology at Edinburgh University and a member of the Medical Research Council, was appointed as the first Vice-Chancellor at the University, which was based in Milton Keynes. Student applications began in 1970 and the first courses got under way in January 1971, utilising a range of new teaching strategies including specially made television programmes, residential schools and home experiment kits.

Bridgewater joined the OU Council in 1975 as a Privy Council nominee and served for six years. Watts helped the University to develop its strategy for its guidance services. The University gradually won over many of its most sceptical critics, devising courses that were recognised internationally for their quality. By 1980 around 6,000 students a year were graduating from the OU and today the number is over 37,000.

A Time to Reassess

By 1974, CRAC's tenth year, there was ample evidence of how the careers education sector as a whole, and CRAC as an integral part of it, had grown and improved over the previous decade. Careers education was now recognised as a valid and important component of the educational process at all stages, and a much expanded range of organisations sought to represent and co-ordinate the activities of its various interested parties.

However, there was little room for complacency, either at sectoral or organisational level. Within two years, in October 1976, James Callaghan, the new Labour Prime Minister, would make a speech at Ruskin College, Oxford, that sparked renewed debate about the underlying purpose of education in terms of each pupil's life span. He observed that:

'The goals of our education, from nursery school through to adult education, are clear enough. It is to equip children to the best of their ability for a lively, constructive place in society and also to fit them to do a job of work.'

He went on to highlight *'complaints from industry that new recruits from schools sometimes do not have the basic tools to do the job required'*. There could be no clearer message that the job of those advancing careers education in Britain was only partially complete. Nor would the task become easier amid rising unemployment levels and the enforced spending cuts that dogged much of the decade.

Against this background, CRAC urgently needed to undertake a fundamental reassessment of its operations.

7
The Management Challenge

By 1974 CRAC's Careers Programme was providing materials and courses for employers, careers advisers, subject teachers and students from the third year of school up to post-graduate level.

A Complete Service
For younger pupils selecting their subjects for the fourth and fifth years there were the *CRAC Careers Record System,* the *Crowley Occupational Interests Blank* and most importantly *Middle School Choice*. Materials then guided students through all the major careers staging posts. For fifth-year students deciding whether to go on to A-levels and which subjects to study, *Upper School Choice* was the key; it also introduced the possibility of leaving school to enter other forms of further education or training, or of going straight into employment. Other materials included the *Connolly Occupational Interests Questionnaire*.

For the sixth former choosing a degree course the *Degree Course Guides* were the vital (and unique) reference source with the introductory *Arts* and *Science Degree Course Choice Guides* as a starting point. The *CRAC/CBI Yearbook of Education and Training Opportunities*, often used alongside the CRAC *Perspective* films, helped the sixth-form leaver to find a suitable starting point, whilst for the student facing a gap between finishing school and beginning university *While You Wait* (successor to *Students in Transition*, another first from CRAC), was the much-needed comprehensive reference guide.

CRAC had also broadened its services by producing *Careers Beyond a Degree*, which showed the links between degree subject and occupations (see p.70), and by launching its 'Undergraduate' and 'Graduate Schools'.

For careers advisers and teachers throughout the country, CRAC had provided the 'Careers Library Index and Card Service', and its broad span of teacher courses covering training in the effective use of specialist careers tools such as PEGS, the *Connolly* and the *Crowley* were very popular.

For subject teachers, who were recognised as having a major influence on students' degree course and career decisions, specialist courses were developed to provide up-to-date information on

From 1973, CRAC materials included comprehensive *Guides* to the entire UK education system, careers education classroom books for 3rd and 4th year pupils and materials for the training and development of careers teachers, all published by Hobsons Press.

developments in their particular school subject fields at degree level, as well as the links between school subjects and non-school subject degree courses. At the same time, employers were encouraged to contribute to CRAC careers programmes and helped to keep up to date with the developments in the schools, colleges and universities that were likely to impact on upcoming cohorts of employees.

Reflection and Review

Thus, ten years of developing and disseminating solutions to meet the careers sector's changing needs had by 1974 produced a comprehensive portfolio of guides, teaching materials and courses. The sheer breadth of its range of resources demanded specialisation of functions requiring publishing skills, teacher training techniques, and career development and research knowledge.

As outlined in earlier chapters, CRAC's publishing had expanded rapidly and sales made a significant contribution to overheads. But other areas of activity were in constant need of financial support, particularly research. For the publishing wing to be able to continue to meet the demand which CRAC itself had created, more working capital would be needed to fund development costs, specialist writers' fees, design costs and increasingly large print runs. CRAC's Council, however, had concerns that heavy borrowings might pose a threat to the organisation's stability. They recognised that a miscalculation of demand for any given title, or a libel or other legal action (perhaps requiring a print run to be pulped), might prove catastrophic. Attempting to compete with the publishing programmes of commercial rivals was, in Bridgewater's words, '*far too risky for a charity*'.

CRAC's not-for-profit status had offered an adequate financial basis for its launch stage, as specific needs of its target audience and marketplace were being defined. It was only when it became apparent that the provision of hard information and attractive presentation were of over-riding importance that the urgent need for outside sources of capital became clear. Fruitless approaches were made to a number of external publishers: even the idea of an arm's-length relationship with CRAC, operating under an exclusive royalties deal, did not appeal to them.

CRAC's only remaining options were either to split off its capital-intensive publishing activities and close them down, or for Bridgewater and other members of the CRAC staff to try and create a separate organisation to develop a publishing business. CRAC's Trustees therefore asked Bridgewater to put forward a business proposition and a three-year plan for a free-standing publishing company, including the

Hobsons Conduit where it was originally erected in Market Hill, Cambridge.
From an 18th Century print

terms and conditions under which this company would acquire CRAC's publishing interests. Sir Mark Turner, a Director of RTZ, and Jack Davies, a Director of the Bank of England, agreed to convene a working party which presented its proposal first to the Trustees and then to the CRAC members after nearly a year's deliberations. Of supreme importance were the twin principles that agreement between CRAC and the new publishing firm should be based upon an 'arms length' contract and that the interests of CRAC should be protected and enhanced.

The final contract was constructed around the right to reproduce the four-letter logotype 'CRAC'. Its design, which was legally registered as the patented property of CRAC, could not be modified or changed, and must always be shown on all the publications which were to be licenced to the new firm, in dimensions as large or larger than the name and logotype of the new firm. A substantial 'up-front' payment was agreed along with a three-year repayment schedule of the balance of the agreed sum, with an interest charge of 9%.

In the first year of the new publishing contract CRAC received £34,620 from the new firm. CRAC's financial situation was transformed; its staff numbers, rent and other overheads were more than halved; and it now had a growing cash reserve.

The Birth of Hobsons

The new company was able to become fully operational almost immediately with three separate divisions, dealing with data gathering, learning materials and recruitment services. Whilst project development and marketing took place in-house with specialist commissioning editors and writers, a large number of freelance consultants were also employed. There was an in-house design studio but print production, warehousing and distribution were all sub-contracted.

Bridgewater resigned as Director of CRAC in 1973 to set up the new firm. A top priority was to decide upon a name which, on the one hand, linked with CRAC's role of advising on choices and, on the other, reflected Cambridge traditions. About 100 yards from CRAC's Bateman Street office stands the beautiful monument presented to Cambridge by the carrier and liveryman, Thomas Hobson, who died in 1630. Hobsons required his customers to take the next available horse, rather than giving them a choice. Hence 'Hobson's Choice'. Enquiries with the Patent Office established that neither the name nor an image of the monument had been registered, so Bridgewater made his choice, Hobsons Press. The strength of the link was confirmed by a chance meeting of the university's Regius Professor of Latin and Bridgewater a matter of days after the new name had been registered:

Professor:*'Hello Bridgewater. What are you doing these days?'*
Bridgewater:*'I've just started to run a company in Cambridge called Hobsons Press.'*
Professor:*'How interesting. Well done! I hadn't realised the old firm was still in business.'*

To provide Hobsons with the finance for the initial payment to CRAC plus the necessary working capital, Robin Ramm, who had been working for RTZ and had since become a freelance adviser to CRAC, invested 26%. The balance was raised by Bridgewater.

Establishing NICEC

Watts was concerned that this restructuring would leave Hobsons with *'all the energy'* whilst the non-commercial aspects of CRAC (including his Research and Development Unit) might become marginalised. There were also fears that funding distribution within CRAC might sideline research altogether. Responding to these worries, it was decided to strengthen CRAC's research arm by establishing a separate research organisation, ideally locating it within a university or other institution with relevant research interests. Watts envisaged an institute for careers education and counselling which would be at the forefront of a career guidance model based on learning and counselling. As noted in Chapter 6, Watts had become increasingly involved in the promotion of counselling, both in career guidance and in wider contexts, particularly through the establishment and development of the Standing Conference for the Advancement of Counselling in 1970. Here he had worked closely with Hans Hoxter, described in Hoxter's obituary in the *Guardian* in 2003 as the *'founding father of the modern counselling movement'* in the UK.

The new institute could not have got off the ground without the guidance and support of Sir Peter Venables, who was Chairman of the Open University and with whom Bridgewater had worked closely during his Trusteeship there. Watts recalled that it was Venables who forcefully argued for a *'National Institute'* rather than an 'institute' or 'unit'. *'Do you want to be a National Institute?'*, he asked. *'Well, I suppose so'*, replied Watts. *'Then call yourself one. If you're good enough, you will become one.' 'It was the best piece of advice I ever had,'* Watts would later recall. It would not be feasible now.

The other key contact was Sir Norman Lindop, the Director of Hatfield Polytechnic, who was a member of one of CRAC's Advisory

Panels. He proved a keen ally and offered to house the Institute at the Polytechnic's Bayfordbury House just outside Hertford, a picturesque old country house that was too far away from main campus to be used regularly for teaching and for which the Polytechnic was keen to find suitable uses. In due course, the Polytechnic made the highly attractive offer of a principal lectureship and two senior lectureships without any teaching responsibilities.

In 1975 the National Institute for Careers Education and Counselling (NICEC) was established with Watts as Executive Director and Bill Law as its first Senior Fellow. The declared aim of the new body was

'to advance the development of guidance services in Britain through a programme of education and training, and of research and development work'.

NICEC was also able to raise £53,000 from the Leverhume Foundation spread over three years with which to finance the appointment of Professor Donald Super from Columbia University, New York, as Honorary Director. Super was widely regarded as the leading world authority in the careers field. He was based in CRAC's Cambridge office and arrangements were made to secure a fellowship for him at Wolfson College, so giving him an additional foothold within the University of Cambridge. Super's stay in NICEC lasted for three years and gave NICEC invaluable international visibility. It culminated in a substantial and trail-blazing academic book, *Career Development in Britain*, edited by Super, Watts and Jenny Kidd, with contributions from other NICEC staff and other leading UK academics in the field.

With its core funding provided jointly by CRAC and Hatfield Polytechnic, NICEC's solid foundations enabled it to tender for and successfully secure substantial research contracts with organisations including the DES, the Schools Council, the Further Education Unit and the Manpower Services Commission. These enabled it to grow its staff to a dozen or more research fellows.

Watts was clear that if NICEC was to establish a lasting independent reputation in the field, it must not be open to any suspicion that its work was influenced by the commercial concerns of Hobsons Press. For this reason, Watts declined to take up shares in Hobsons. Also, NICEC won a contract with the Schools Council to disseminate its Careers Education and Guidance Project (whose materials had been published by Longmans), providing affirmation of NICEC's independence. The support of CRAC and Hobsons in its taking on this contract was a clear sign of maturing relationships between the three entities.

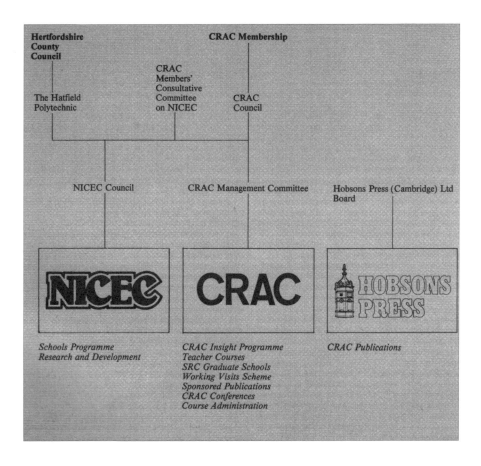

Hertfordshire
County
Council

CRAC Membership

CRAC
Members'
Consultative
Committee
on NICEC

The Hatfield
Polytechnic

CRAC
Council

NICEC Council

CRAC Management Committee

Hobsons Press (Cambridge) Ltd
Board

Schools Programme
Research and Development

CRAC Insight Programme
Teacher Courses
SRC Graduate Schools
Working Visits Scheme
Sponsored Publications
CRAC Conferences
Course Administration

CRAC Publications

A chart showing the relationships between the three organisations. Reproduced from the CRAC *Journal.*

A flexible and fast-moving organisation

Thus, in just over ten years, the activities originally envisaged by CRAC had required a radically new structure: CRAC, Hobsons, NICEC and IMS, as the diagram opposite illustrates

IMS had been set up as a specialist institute within Sussex University. Hobsons was now the careers materials publisher; NICEC was doing the research and development work; and CRAC itself was administering its Schools Programme and other training projects including the Undergraduate and Graduate Schools and the Britain Australia Vocational Exchange (BAVE) Scheme, whilst managing the relationships between the various operations. CRAC had been notable in its first ten years for its innovation, its rapid growth, and its ability to respond to client needs and opportunities in the new careers sector. The organisation had only survived and grown because it had constantly re-examined and changed its methods of meeting evolving needs in a rapidly changing environment.

CRAC's not-for-profit status had been important for its initial recognition and success. But within its first three years it had identified the importance of manpower research and had enabled the creation of IMS within a separate structure without becoming distracted from CRAC's core vision by its day-to-day management. When, a year later, Tony Watts had jumped ship to do postgraduate studies at the University of York, this left the core CRAC organisation with two very different areas of activity – courses and conferences for teachers and students on the one hand and publications development on the other – but no research function. The skills and personalities needed for these two remaining areas were very different and there were signs of tensions between the two.

In addition, growing success was imposing growing financial pressures. In the sixth year of CRAC's history, at about the time that Watts returned from York, the pressures were resolved by the RTZ loan and the business was analysed by Robin Ramm. The separation of the publishing activity from the remaining core CRAC services followed fairly quickly.

Complementary Nests

Without formal recognition or a once-and-for-all decision, the delivery of the original core CRAC objective had been segmented into specialist groups. Why had this happened? There were obvious financial considerations but other motivations exerted their pressures. The research group demanded intellectual probity free of commercial pressures, whilst the publishing group, facing the uncharted waters of business competition, needed the freedom to innovate. Klaus Boehm, who had master-minded the IMS development, saw the need for a separate research group which could focus solely on complex issues of manpower supply and demand; he also had a personal career agenda which CRAC was unlikely to be able to provide. CRAC's flexibility and ability to sub-divide itself into free-standing units, each with the same fundamental aim but each offering solutions requiring an appropriate setting for their fulfillment, had caused CRAC to develop a concept of 'complementary nests' from each of which many more eggs were able to be laid and hatched than would have been possible from a single 'nest'.

8
The Separate 'Nests'

1 CRAC: The Original 'Nest'

Steadying the Ship

Its 1973 restructure left CRAC with a core staff of just five to face the challenge of redefining its role. John Brodie moved from the Scottish Office down to Cambridge to take up the post of Director, with a remit to stabilise the organisation in this transitional period. Of taking up the post, Brodie said:

> '*I was keen to come down but I can't say it wasn't intimidating as I had to learn new tricks, meet new people and so on. But at least I was well steeped in the ways of CRAC before I got there.*'

As well as ensuring the continued functioning of the Conference Programme, the Tube Investments Business Education Unit, the Undergraduate Schools and the Graduate Schools, Brodie did much to strengthen the British-Australian Vocational Exchange (BAVE) scheme. This programme, which annually provided about 250 young Britons and Australians with two months' work-experience placements in their other country, followed by a month in which they could travel, was administered by Susan McPhater. The programme had been running since 1963 under the aegis of the English-Speaking Union and in 1970 Peter Spanoghe, then Chairman of CRAC, had negotiated a management contract for its administration. The Australian government provided free airline tickets as the country was actively encouraging an inflow of skilled workers from abroad. There was also significant industrial support particularly from mining companies, including BHP and RTZ, who considered the scheme an important means of encouraging graduates to join their companies.

Spiralling unemployment in the mid- to late-1970s had highlighted the ongoing poor links between employers and educational institutions. CRAC's long-established Undergraduate Schools offered a blueprint for improving relations and understanding between the two sectors. With new government funding available, the decision was taken in 1978 to employ David Blandford, a visiting tutor for the Graduate Schools since 1969, as a full-time manager to oversee these programmes and to establish the Insight Programme and a special Insight Project Appeal Fund.

'Insight' was the re-branded name of the 'Undergraduate Schools' and also extended the principle of insights into management to sixth-formers and to their teachers too. The need to reach teachers as well as students was heightened by the ending of the Tube Investments funding. Blandford was tasked to find five or six industrial partners who would each provide £5,000 core financing per year. After nine months in the post, less than half of this core funding had materialised; as Blandford's salary relied upon it, there was a minor crisis before Shell, Unilever and P&O, amongst others, came up with significant support. Blandford's successful lobbying of the Department of Trade and Industry (DTI) generated powerful support from Dr Eric Bates, head of the DTI's newly formed Industry-Education Unit, from which annual funding of £20,000 was provided, thus solving the problem.

In 1979 the Thatcher administration set up an industry and education advisory committee in a bid to improve links between educators and employers as a long-term response to the impact of Callaghan's Ruskin speech three years earlier. Bates oversaw its setting-up and the publication of a periodical which proved to be valuable for promoting CRAC's activities. Bates had been employed by ICI before moving to the DTI and proved a good friend to CRAC over the ensuing years, strengthened by his links via ICI with Dr Duncan Davies, an early supporter of the 'Undergraduate Schools' and originator of the 'Graduate Schools'.

The 'Insight Appeal Fund' finally succeeded with modified financial arrangements whereby employers paid a full economic fee for the young managers they sent on the courses, making independent grants in aid of CRAC's core programme.

Brodie left in 1979 to take up a position in Glasgow with the CBI's Education Foundation to run its new Understanding British Industry project. CRAC's 'unearned' income was now derived largely from Hobsons' royalties and from donations from about fifty employer members. Its funding was secure.

A Focus on the Conference Programme

Brodie was succeeded by Alan Jamieson, who came from an educational publishing background which included working as a history and careers master and as an educational programme producer for the BBC before an editorship with Penguin Books. Jamieson saw that by growing CRAC's courses and conference programme, the organisation's finances and viability could rapidly be enhanced. He had a keen understanding of the pressing issues of the day and was able to construct conferences and events around them, drawing expert speakers from government, schools, universities and employers. His emphasis was mostly on higher education questions and in particular the debate surrounding the funding and relative status of universities and polytechnics. Although he pursued some government contract work, he transformed CRAC's programme so that conference fees became a main source of income. A particularly important conference on the development of the higher education sector was addressed by Sir Keith Joseph, the then Secretary of State for Education, whose appearance guaranteed a much over-subscribed event.

'Enterprise' had become the buzzword of the new Conservative administration and CRAC provided a neutral platform for discussions between government, commercial leaders, vice chancellors, heads of careers services and the like. But Jamieson's tenure was short and he left in 1981 to become Director of Business Studies at Hertford College. However, his relationship with CRAC endured and for the next five years or so he worked as a conference consultant, was appointed to the Hobsons board in 1987 and was responsible for commissioning or authoring some of Hobsons' best-selling CRAC books including *Your Choice of A-Levels*, *Your Choice of Degrees and Diplomas* and *Which Career?*.

The Fourth CRAC Director
David Blandford put his name forward as a candidate for the CRAC Directorship in 1981 and succeeded in the selection process. Inevitably, CRAC's courses and conferences could only accommodate a limited number of participants and Blandford faced the problem of extending CRAC's influence without excessively increasing overheads. He continued to secure significant state funding, winning finance on a conference-by-conference sponsorship basis. He sought more donations and practical help from employers too, particularly for the 'Insight Programme', developing custom-made course materials such as *The Pampers Nappy Case Study* with Procter & Gamble. These could then be sold to institutions to run their own courses independently from CRAC. In this way, CRAC disseminated its message to a wider number of people whilst also bolstering its own funds. CRAC also managed a series of events devised by NICEC, with CRAC managing logistics whilst NICEC prepared programme content and subsequent reports. The best known and longest running of these was 'Admissions to Higher Education' which had originally been devised by CRAC but was now revised and restructured each year by NICEC.

'Learning for a Changing World'
The Thatcher government overhauled the school curriculum, increasing

emphasis on developing skills for the world of work. In this climate, the 'Insight' model was adapted to give teachers the skills to teach business knowledge to their pupils. BP provided tens of thousands of pounds every year for such projects in local authority areas where it had refineries, and CRAC secured BP's backing for its 'Learning for a Changing World' teacher in-service training project. Launched in 1984 in Essex and Hertfordshire, the project consisted of an initial two-day CRAC-run course, followed by six months of in-school work and then a one-day debriefing session. Later courses were run in Wales and Scotland, and the Ford Motor Company joined BP as sponsors. The project materials were collected together by CRAC and made available for sale to schools through Hobsons, again extending the potential influence of the scheme without financially overburdening CRAC.

1986 was designated 'Industry Year' by the Government, the culmination of a decade of rumination instigated by the Ruskin speech. CRAC's showpiece event in July was a conference called 'Education and Change: Can You Afford to Ignore It?', held at Churchill College, Cambridge. Investigating the current state of and future developments in the relationship between education and industry, it re-emphasised the need for ever closer collaboration. In the same year CRAC's turnover reached £1 million for the first time.

In 1987 CRAC moved to its current home, Sheraton House in Cambridge, and Hobsons achieved a full listing on the London Stock Exchange. This had been preceded by the complete separation of CRAC and Hobson's 'back office' services and pension schemes. By the time CRAC celebrated its silver anniversary in 1989, Hobsons was generating licence fees and royalties for CRAC of some £45,000 per year.

Preparing for the Millennium

In a climate of growing support for cross-curricular careers development, CRAC developed its first major Training and Enterprise Council conference on 'Education/Business Partnerships' in 1990. CRAC also increased its international reach by running an 'Insight' course in Bruges in 1992 for sixty students from thirty universities and six countries, and five years later developed a Graduate Schools programme with the French government.

The 1990s, though, were difficult for the organisation. After NICEC's physical and financial removal from the University of Hertfordshire in 1992, CRAC undertook to underwrite the continued existence of NICEC, guaranteeing funding for Watts and his Cambridge base as well as the salary of one of its Senior Fellows, Ruth Hawthorn. Within two years CRAC found itself in financial turmoil. Blandford was sure that, at the very least, CRAC could maintain NICEC and the conference programme, but there was the real possibility of losing the Insight and Graduate School programmes. CRAC was in fact able to retain all of these programmes, although the Insight programme was run down after 2000. Having secured a future for CRAC, Blandford retired in 1996 and Donald McGregor was appointed Director.

With a growing focus on lifelong career development, CRAC developed careers initiatives with the Department for Education and Employment (in association with McDonalds restaurants) for children of primary school age and in 1998 held a series of seminars on 'Lifelong Learning'. It also contributed a series of national consultative documents relating to careers education and guidance to the Review of 16-19 Qualifications led by Sir Ron Dearing, and to evaluations of education and employer partnership activities.

In 2002 Donald McGregor was succeeded by David Thomas. By 2003, CRAC's turnover had reached £4 million per year.

CRAC Today

Jeffrey Defries took over as Chief Executive in 2006, and CRAC continues its work in student and professional development and consultancy. With careers education now a long-established feature on the policy agenda and the sector well-populated with private and public enterprises, CRAC faces an ongoing challenge to redefine itself and maintain its relevance.

CRAC's role in relation to education continues to evolve. Its conference on support for career decisions and university admissions at age 18 maintains its position as the pre-eminent national conference in the field, previously *Admissions to Higher Education* and recently retitled *Decisions at 18* to reflect the wide variety of pathways now available to young adults. Insight into Management courses are now firmly embedded in many universities. In the postgraduate sector, CRAC leads *VITAE*, a national programme to accelerate the career and personal development of postgraduate research students and early-career research staff, working in partnership with university-based hubs, funded by Research Councils UK. CRAC's role is to provide innovation, research and support for university-based training staff, foster the sharing of practice and to build a national evidence base demonstrating the impact of the activity on researchers and the research sector.

In 2009 CRAC launched *iCould*, a novel, free online resource comprising a thousand films of personal career stories told by individuals across the entire occupational and social spectrum, aimed at inspiring young people to think about their own career possibilities. *iCould* exemplifies CRAC's continued desire to innovate in the careers world, using the contemporary media used by young people to offer a powerful and inspirational array of content, complementing institutionalised careers support.

CRAC continues its role in research and development in career-related learning, including research for Government on the flow of graduates into science, technology and engineering (notably still an issue for national policy, four decades later).

Despite the organisation's much-changed structure, its fundamental aims remain firmly rooted in those established in 1964.

2 ECCTIS: The Information-Gathering 'Nest'

By the mid-1980s, gathering degree course information from the universities and colleges had become increasingly difficult. New publishers were coming into the field and demanding course information to suit their particular publications, so registrars' departments were becoming over-burdened. As a solution the Department of Education gave a contract to the Open University to provide a central course information service. This was named ECCTIS and had been running, not altogether satisfactorily, under the OU when Bridgewater found out that the original contract and a subsequent three-year renewal had been awarded to the OU without competitive tender. For two years he lobbied relevant Ministers, MPs and Departments, insisting that the ECCTIS contract must go out to public tender. In 1990 a tendering process was finally agreed after vigorous negotiations with Robert Jackson, Under-Secretary of State for Higher Education. With The Times Supplement Ltd and UCAS (each holding 30%) and CRAC (holding 10%), Bridgewater, with the 30% Hobsons share, landed the successful bid and in 1991 set up a new company, ECCTIS 2000 Ltd, to deliver the contract. Thereby, the flow of detailed course information to CRAC/Hobsons publications, including *Degree Course Guides* and *Graduate Studies*, was secured.

The primary task was to administer a national database containing over 100,000 further and higher education courses (CRAC's role within the consortium was to provide evaluation of the service). Within four years the service was fully self-funding (having previously been 70% funded by the state), providing information to 750,000 students via 4,300 CD-Rom access points. In 1994 the contract was renewed for a further ten years. Today ECCTIS Ltd holds the 'NARIC' contract offering comparative information on overseas qualifications, promoting British qualifications abroad, running the 'National Reference Point for Vocational Qualifications', and representing the UK in the European Network of Reference Centres for Vocational Qualifications in the EU Member States.

3 NICEC: The Research and Development 'Nest'

Watts's vision for NICEC was that it should be concerned with careers education and counselling in terms of theory, policy and practice. NICEC's early projects were mostly schools-based. One of its first commissions, in 1975-76, was 'Approaches to Careers Education in Schools', funded by the Church of England Board of Education. This study of six schools resulted in Law and Watts developing their 'DOTS' model, described on the *Graduate Prospects* website as '*probably the best known model of the guidance and career choice process in the UK*'. It has also been influential internationally. The model is composed of four elements: Self-awareness (in career-related terms); Opportunity awareness; Decision learning; and Transition learning (how to implement decisions and deal with the consequences). It remains a much used framework, incorporating later adaptations by Law to recognise the changing working environment.

NICEC also continued its work with the Schools Council on developing and disseminating curriculum materials, as well as serving as a project partner to the Departments of Education and Science, Employment, and Trade and Industry, and to the Manpower Services Commission. By the late 1970s it was involved in several international studies of curriculum provision, working for organisations including UNESCO and the European Commission.

The growth of youth training and opportunities, heralded by the election of the Thatcher government, saw an expansion of programmes concerned with young people in transition between education and work. NICEC was active on several related projects such as 'Guidance and Support in the Youth Opportunities Programme (YOP)' (1980–81) and the 'Youth Training Scheme (YTS) Guidance Development Project' (1982–84). Watts was a member of the MSC's groups which designed YOP and YTS. NICEC also undertook several investigations into education–industry relationships and, in particular, work experience schemes, working closely with the Schools Council Industry Project.

Democratising Careers
NICEC continued to be active in the higher education field (for instance,

Watts and Ruth Hawthorn's study *Guidance Aspects of the Enterprise in Higher Education Programme* from 1990–92). However, while this was strong CRAC territory, NICEC, in Watts's words, was actively seeking to '*democratise the concept of careers*', which meant catering for markets other than the now relatively well-served higher education sector. There were several NICEC studies into guidance services for adults, resulting in influential publications such as Watts's *Counselling at Work* (1977) and one of the first major conferences in the UK on career guidance for adults.

With unemployment rising in the early- and mid-1980s, NICEC examined its impact on careers education in schools and further/adult education, producing teaching materials that portrayed careers decisions as influenced not only by the individual but by political and economic realities beyond their control. Watts's book *Education, Unemployment and the Future of Work,* published by the Open University Press in 1983, was nominated for the Standing Conference on Studies in Education Book Prize. Its four scenarios – the unemployment scenario, the leisure scenario, the employment scenario, and the work scenario – were subsequently used with due attribution by Charles Handy for the final chapter of his book *The Future of Work.*

NICEC was a pioneer in the use of technology in careers education provision and in the late-1980s and early-1990s was closely involved in the development and evaluation of the PROSPECT system, a pioneering DES project to introduce a computer-aided careers guidance system for higher education and sixth-form institutions. NICEC worked with the Manpower Services Commission and the Unit for the Development of Continuing Adult Education on Training Access Points (TAP), which were computerised databases of training opportunities. In later years Watts's team worked with Learndirect on its telephone information service and was quick to embrace internet technology too.

From Organisation to Network

NICEC restructured in 1992 when its relationship ended with Hatfield Polytechnic (which became the University of Hertfordshire in that year). Sir Norman Lindop had handed over to new directors who, whilst remaining supportive of NICEC's work, reduced core funding and ultimately required the organisation to cover all of its own costs. That demand prompted NICEC to withdraw gracefully from the partnership. NICEC had originally been set up as a joint activity of CRAC and Hatfield, with the Polytechnic providing two-thirds of the core financial support. Supplemented by project funding, this had allowed NICEC to employ up to fifteen academic staff and up to a further five support staff. After the break with Hatfield, CRAC agreed to finance Watts and his Cambridge office and to underwrite Hawthorn's work. Of the other two Senior Fellows, Law opted to become a freelance consultant and writer, whilst John Killeen remained on the Hatfield payroll with increased teaching responsibilities: both maintained their roles in NICEC.

Watts was adamant that the organisation needed to retain a higher education partner and established a link with the University of London's Institute of Education, locating Hawthorn there. This link included placing NICEC's uniquely well-stocked library at the Institute. But Watts and his colleagues decided that rather than try to establish a new home with an extensive permanent staff, NICEC should instead become a virtual network based on more fluid relationships between fellows with expertise in as many and varied areas of careers guidance as possible. The network was extended to include specialists in every level of education, as well as in relation to employers, unions and the voluntary and community sector. This structural transition was greatly aided by the contribution of Sir Christopher Ball, the then chair of the NICEC Council, who oversaw a thorough review of how the new structure would work.

Influencing Policy

Striving to frame issues in policy terms, NICEC has throughout its existence sought to maintain strong relations with relevant government departments and civil servants. Whilst careers guidance necessarily prioritises the individual, NICEC has striven to show how this private good converts into a public good, with benefits for the economy and society at large. It has thus tried to influence public policy through consultation but also by analysis and critical evaluation of the mechanisms in place. From the mid-1990s through to the new millennium, NICEC hosted a number of 24-hour policy consultations designed in partnership with and funded by government departments, which were then followed by a brief NICEC-authored report. Its independent status provided the opportunity for close involvement with policy-making whilst at the same time allowing for non-partisan criticism and analysis. NICEC's structure granted it no power but allowed for it to act as an influential catalytic organisation.

In 1996 five of NICEC's principal figures – Watts, Law, Killeen, Hawthorn and Jennifer Kidd – collaborated on a major book entitled *Rethinking Careers Education and Guidance: Theory, Policy and Practice*. Supported by funding from the Esmée Fairbairn Charitable

Trust, it provided a synthesis of NICEC's core work and highlighted the relationship between theory, policy and practice, each of which, according to Watts, *'has to be illuminated by the others'*. The book remains the standard text in the field.

Eggs in the NICEC Nest

When the relationship with the Institute of Education came to an end in 1997, the NICEC library moved to the University of Derby, where Watts accepted a visiting professorship and helped to establish the Centre for Guidance Studies (led by Deirdre Hughes), an organisation based in certain respects on the NICEC model and which may legitimately be seen as another of CRAC's 'eggs'. Two years earlier NICEC had played a role in incubating another 'egg': the Guidance Council, a joint project of the Royal Society for the Encouragement of the Arts, Manufactures and Commerce (RSA) and the CBI. It was launched through a conference addressed by Sir Christopher Ball on behalf of the RSA, Sir Bryan Nicholson on behalf of the CBI, and Watts, and through a subsequent letter in the *Times* signed by the three of them. Sir Christopher Ball was its first chair and the Council operated successfully until its dissolution in 2006, during which time it was a significant influence on several major initiatives including the Learndirect careers helpline and the Matrix quality standards designed to cover all guidance provision.

Watts left as Director of NICEC in 2001, a year ahead of schedule, to take up a position with the OECD in Paris as co-director of a 14-country Career Guidance Policy Review. Its project model was subsequently extended by the World Bank, the European Commission and the European Training Foundation to cover 55 countries, including the West Balkans and the Middle East, with Watts closely involved in all the reviews. He also played a significant role in the initiation of a biennial series of international symposia on career development and public policy, held in three different continents from 1999, and in the establishment of the International Centre for Career Development and Public Policy – yet another 'egg'.

Following his period at OECD, Watts returned to Cambridge, to work as an international policy consultant. He retained his links with NICEC, and was given the honorific title of Founding Fellow and Life President. He also retained his visiting professorship at the University of Derby, to which he added a further visiting professorship at Canterbury Christ Church University. He has been awarded honorary degrees by the Open University, the University of Derby and Edinburgh Napier University, and an OBE for his services to education.

NICEC, meanwhile, remains an active network of fellows, although it has been reinstituted to become a separate legal entity wholly-owned by CRAC. Its current Chair is Allister McGowan.

4 HOBSONS: The Publishing 'Nest'

Hobsons had been separated from CRAC in 1974 and incorporated as a limited company. From the point of view of CRAC's Council the logic had been entirely clear, but the over-riding issue was to conduct a fair, arms-length negotiation which would lead to a strengthening of CRAC's finances and an on-going relationship. The final Agreement hung upon a licence for Hobsons to have the exclusive right to use the CRAC logotype on all its careers-related publications. The Agreement held unbroken for over 30 years, during which time Hobsons provided a solid flow of 'unearned income' through royalties and licence fees to sustain CRAC's work, averaging £20k a year at 1969 values.

Hobsons' publishing strategy had three strands:

a) the provision of comprehensive data on courses and careers

b) the development of classroom teaching materials for careers education and also for other relevant subjects, and

c) the development of guidance materials for professional use.

Hobsons were pioneers in the field of data collection and processing and were producing their 1,000-page annual course directories using 'single stroke' keyboarding in the early' 70s – long before these techniques had reached Fleet Street or the Hansard writers in the House of Commons. In this work they were fortunate to have colleagues in the University of Cambridge who used CRAC/Hobsons publications to trial their very early electronic devices and also to have a computer-literate Director, Robin Ramm, to exploit the new technology and keep Hobsons ahead of the competition. In 1987-88 Hobsons published 47 directories.

To develop its careers education materials Hobsons worked very closely with a small number of teachers, leaders in the field, to turn their expertise in the classroom into materials which could disseminate their skills very widely. Michael Smith, Head of Filton High School, and Geoffrey Cooksey, Director of the Stantonbury Campus, were two of the Company's most prolific and distinguished authors. Their books could not have been produced without the support and expertise of Hobsons' in-house editors.

Nearly the last and by far the largest of Hobsons' schools projects were *Microelectronics for All* and *Race for Technologists*, the latter of which dealt with the application of fibre-optic technology as a new means of communication and won the Didacta Prize in 1991. The first of these kits was designed by the Microelectronics Education Programme to teach 11- to 14-year-old pupils how a computer worked; Hobsons won its publishing contract. The second was designed and developed by Hobsons.

By 1987 Hobsons had a turnover of over £5m, and published 116 totally new or fully revised books and directories in that year. A Hobsons report of the time stated:

'*The multiplicity of course and career choices and options facing students, their parents, advisers and teachers would be impossible to unravel without Hobsons' databases, directories and guides – and learning materials on the art of decision-making itself.*'

Turnover in 1988 grew to £6.5m and £8.4m in 1989. But in 1990, due to the 'gross professional negligence' of a firm of financial advisers, the company was defrauded of over £1m in an acquisition and the Directors were forced to recommend the sale of the company in 1991. Bridgewater stayed on with the purchasers, DMGT, until 1993, when he resigned on a strategic issue. He was able to take with him a publication in the field of information about elderly care which he subsequently developed into a successful company, Care Choices Ltd, of which he is a director. He remains a director of ECCTIS, which is now solely owned by Hobsons. He is also a director of his daughter's pottery company, Emma Bridgewater Ltd., and deputy chairman of Papworth Trust, a charity concerned with disability.

Hobsons sold off its educational publishing business and its recruitment directory publishing business. Today along with its ECCTIS/NARIC interests Hobsons (still owned by DMGT) is pioneering in the field of university and college student enrolement and retention *'empowering the educational professional'* using systems originating in the USA and now widely used in the UK.

5 IMS: The Manpower Forecasting 'Nest'

Originally set up to provide research-based information to the Government and employers on manpower flows and policies under its first director, Michael Hall (who had formerly been at Esso and had worked on manpower planning at the LSE), the Institute in its formative stages had close links with CRAC, including supplying it with relevant labour market information. Klaus Boehm, who had been its Secretary and a Senior Fellow running education and training and publications, left the Institute after some five years to become a consultant editor in academic publishing. In 1994 its name was changed to the Institute of Employment Studies.

In 2008 IES celebrated its 40th anniversary as the UK's leading independent centre of research and consultancy in employment policy and HR practice. It contributes to corporate strategy and performance, through research and evidence-based consultancy by individual employers. IES is also commissioned by government departments, agencies and other bodies to research and advise on the effectiveness and development of public employment policy. Its expertise is available to all organisations through research, consultancy, publications and the internet.

Adrian Bridgewater in the early 1970s.

Tony Watts in the early 1970s.

Bridgewater with Sir Keith Joseph, Secretary of State for Education and Science, at CRAC's 21st Anniversary Dinner in 1985.

9
The Sum of Its Parts

The term 'social enterprise' first came into common usage in a British context in the late 1970s, principally through the writings of Freer Spreckley (who later established the UK Social Enterprise Partnership Ltd). In *Social Audit – A Management Tool for Co-operative Working*, she gave this definition:

'*An enterprise that is owned by those who work in it and/or reside in a given locality, is governed by registered social as well as commercial aims and objectives and run co-operatively may be termed a social enterprise.*'

Alternatively, Rob Paton (in *Managing and Measuring Social Enterprise*) described a social enterprise as:

'*Most simply, an organisation where people have to be business-like, but are not in it for the money.*'

A third take is offered by Peter Brinckerhoff in *Social Entrepreneurship: The Art of Mission-Based Venture Development*:

'*You need to think of your entire organisation as a business "with a heart,"… but one that is business-like, uses business techniques to pursue its mission, and worries about the bottom line, both in terms of finance and mission.*'

While pre-dating the term 'social enterprise' by almost two decades, CRAC conformed to these defining characteristics. The 1960s and 1970s was a period of sustained development, both in society at large and in the careers field specifically, providing an exciting climate in which individuals and organisations could instigate change. But CRAC's early years of rapid expansion and energetic innovation continue to provide a number of lessons for social enterprises looking to start-up or expand now, lessons that maintain their relevance beyond their particular historical moment.

A Clear Mission
Brinckerhoff argues that:

'*Everything in a not-for-profit starts and ends with mission. It's the reason you exist, and it is your ultimate product.*'

In CRAC's case, the organisation emerged out of a social need that had been identified by Bridgewater and Watts in their time at Cornmarket Press: namely, the lack of comprehensive and accurate information that students required to make balanced decisions about their future educational and career paths. The Robbins Report, with its demand for an expansion of the higher education sector to meet national needs, shone a clear light on the vastly inadequate supply of information that was destined only to become worse as the numbers of educational institutions and courses mushroomed.

With the need unmet, vast numbers of young people faced being without the basic tools to make life-defining decisions. Drawing on their experience of researching and supplying information in this area, CRAC's founders could see how they might be able to extend their activities to satisfy this need. From its outset CRAC had a clear sense of what it wanted to achieve, beyond the simple bottom-line profitability goal of a regular business. Its initial aims encapsulated its agenda:

a) to help all careers advisers in schools, colleges, the universities and the Youth Employment Service;

b) to provide an information link between education and employment.

These underlying principles – acting as a bridge between the worlds of education and employment – subsequently informed all of CRAC's activities, from early innovations like the *Course Comparison Guides* and the Question Service, via long-running projects such as the Undergraduate Schools and Graduate Schools, through to more recent innovations such as iCould. With a well-defined vision of what they wanted to achieve, the CRAC management were able to evaluate each new project against its chances of meeting these goals.

It is not enough for a social enterprise to have a vague notion of wanting to do good. To work effectively and efficiently, it must have a coherent set of ambitious with achievable goals. In the rapidly-changing educational environment of early-1960s Britain, the founders of CRAC defined just such a set of goals that have retained their relevance to the present day.

Building a Solid Financial Base

CRAC began operations in 1964, seeking to deliver social goals in a businesslike and efficient way. When Brickerhoff was writing at the turn of the twenty-first century, nearly 40 years later, he argued that '*... being "businesslike" is still controversial in a mission-based organisation*'. One of CRAC's most critical achievements was that it grasped so early that working in the context of a solid financial framework was not incompatible with its social goals; rather, delivering those goals was reliant upon it. As Brickerhoff argues:

'The reason you, your staff, and board take entrepreneurial risks is to get more mission out the door, sooner, better, and in a more focused manner.'

While not all of CRAC's activities were individually self-sustaining (virtually an impossibility in any social enterprise), the organisation as a whole had to be. The alternative was to carry out a few socially-valuable projects over a short period of time before financially combusting. By striving for economic sustainability, CRAC gave itself the optimum chance of providing the most number of people over the longest period of time with the best quality of service. Making money out of those projects that can be profitable, and selectively reinvesting profits to support those which will not, is essential for the longevity of a social enterprise.

With early consultancy advice CRAC became highly effective at maximising profitability and keeping risk within reasonable margins. For instance, they quickly won the CBI *Card Index* contract to give CRAC's finances an early fillip, helping to keep the organisation afloat when other operations, like the Question Service, were eating up finance. Over time CRAC's track-record in delivering high-quality publications and courses allowed for the creation of a portfolio of services for which fair fees could be charged from those who could reasonably pay. Examples from a much longer list include the *Degree Course Guides* and *Graduate Employment and Training*, the Interview Skills programme, the Undergraduate Schools and Graduate Schools, all of which proved to be profitable over many years.

CRAC also learned quickly how to secure alternative funding sources for projects which were not necessarily profitable but were important to meeting its wider social goals. By creating services that *were* profitable and by ensuring a professional approach at all times, the management team was able to win the confidence of funders. From the £500 per year guaranteed by the Society of Drapers in 1965 and the CRAC Appeal Fund that earned in excess of £30,000, CRAC's businesslike approach persuaded potential investors that CRAC was a sensible and worthwhile recipient of finance. It secured significant core funding, often on a project-by-project basis, from a range of major industrial partners (e.g. BP, Shell, Unilever, Procter & Gamble) as well as charitable foundations and government departments with an interest in the careers field. Allied to this, CRAC benefited from its 'eye for a bargain', with which for example, it had secured office space at well below market rates.

One of the keys to success is that a social enterprise remain realistic about its financial situation and moves early to meet any emerging problems. With this in mind, CRAC took several difficult financial decisions at appropriate times. For instance, with its accounts under major strain at the end of the 1960s, the management team took on the burden (under advice) of a £50,000 loan from RTZ. Rather than suffer further financial strain by undertaking a long programme of debt repayment, CRAC instigated a comprehensive review of its financial systems, got back on to an even keel and had repaid the debt within a year and a half.

Similarly hard decisions were taken in 1973–74 when it had become clear that the major expansion of CRAC's publishing activities (reflecting success in meeting its core aims) would put the organisation's finances under severe pressure, whilst the legal framework of CRAC was hindering further publishing growth. This led to the landmark decision to separate publishing operations out from CRAC's other activities, with the newly-formed Hobsons taking up the reins. What might have signalled the end of CRAC as an expansive body in fact led to its rejuvenation. Within a year NICEC had been established and CRAC was focusing on its other core activities, buoyed by the benefits of an ongoing royalty agreement with Hobsons.

A social enterprise cannot afford to be embarrassed to make profits where it can, nor to be unrealistic about which projects will not recover costs. Risk is inevitable in any entrepreneurial enterprise but should be minimised through good governance and what Brickerhoff calls '... *the use of established business development practices to keep that risk reasonable*'. Profit must remain a fundamental target because, as he also notes:

'*... without profit, there is no money for innovation, and without innovation, an organisation withers on the vine.*'

Innovation Works Best on a Blank Sheet of Paper

With a clear vision of its aims and a sound grasp of its finances, CRAC's early years were ones of rapid organic growth, marked by a willingness to experiment and a refusal to be constrained by preconceived ideas. This was based upon the ability of its staff firstly to identify new and emerging problems within the careers sector that needed to be solved and, secondly, to recognise opportunities to provide a solution and to act upon them. CRAC aimed to be a bridge between education and the world of work. As with bridges both physical and metaphorical, its inherent flexibility and responsiveness to changing conditions was fundamental to its enduring strength.

CRAC was never a site of quiet consensus but an environment in which new ideas could be voiced and tested, with the best allowed to take seed. This ethos stemmed from Bridgewater and Watts, who were united in their broad common mission but often came at it from widely different places. If left unchecked, this situation might have led to divisions, but both enjoyed the exchange of ideas and each recognised their own weaknesses and the other's strengths. Alan Jamieson remembered:

'CRAC's vitality came because of the union of two disparate personalities: Tony Watts - academically directed, thoughtful, an original thinker in careers education; and Adrian Bridgewater - dynamic, superb personal skills, commercially astute and aware. There were sparks but they always resolved them. Unique!'

Furthermore, they built up networks of contacts with a diverse range of interests and skills which ensured the organisation had an intellectually versatile basis. CRAC's founders utilised relationships forged at Cambridge and at Cornmarket (where they had considerable access to leading educationalists and industrialists throughout the country) to generate initial support for their project, to staff CRAC, its Council and Advisory Panel, and to secure funding. Early supporters in the press were cultivated to give the best opportunity of spreading the word about CRAC's operations. As more contacts were 'converted' to the cause, these converts brought with them yet more new networks of potentially valuable contacts.

CRAC entered the market with a small but well-thought-out portfolio of services, based around market research conducted informally among their personal networks and more formally through mechanisms such as the Schools Survey. As Brickerhoff has argued:

'Social entrepreneurs must be market-sensitive while still being mission-based. To do that, you have to regularly ask your markets (the people you serve, as well as the people who fund you) what they want.'

From an initial membership package consisting of four issues of the *Journal*, access to the Question Service and six or seven Information Sheets, a range of new services soon emerged which in turn generated many more. So, for instance, the early idea of Information Sheets offering comparative analysis of the higher education options available in a given subject was well received, leading to a series of *Course Comparisons*, which were later repackaged and sold at considerable profit as the *Degree Course Guides*. The *Journal*, meanwhile, provided a forum through which research projects - like that into the interim between school and university - could be disseminated and built upon. That particular study, for instance, was developed into a booklet which became one of CRAC's best-selling publications.

Meanwhile, the Undergraduate Schools evolved as a solution to a problem that became ever more apparent from CRAC's early work: the failure in communication between undergraduates and employers. The Undergraduate Schools were in turn influential on other projects such as the Graduate Schools and the 'Interview Skills'courses. The overhaul of CRAC's library system led to the creation of the nationally-employed CLCI classification system and programmes such as 'Libraries on a Shoestring'. A visit to Gerd Sommerhoff's innovative science department at Sevenoaks School prompted the production of the *Creativity in School* film to disseminate this example of good practice, which then inspired the *Perspectives* documentaries series. The list goes on.

As well as a process whereby one CRAC project might precipitate the creation of several others, the organisation was also highly responsive to problems highlighted outside its own infrastructure. The Graduate Schools, for instance, were in large part a response to the Swann Report's findings into the flow (or lack thereof) of science graduates into industry. Similarly, the growing uptake of Business Studies as a school subject gave impetus to the creation of CRAC's Tube Investments-sponsored Business Studies Unit. A consistent openness to ideas and ability to respond quickly and effectively underpinned CRAC's ability to meet its key goals.

Re-evaluating the Aims and the Means

When a social enterprise begins to fulfill its goals, there is a temptation for it to keep doing the same thing, but that can only lead to its stagnation. Once CRAC achieved some early momentum it chose to intensify its programme of developing new services, searching out and seizing new opportunities. It was thus able to ensure it remained relevant in a rapidly changing sphere of activity.

Brickerhoff argues for the need to continue progressing as follows:

'Steady, consistent improvement in services and the constant adding to the value of those services from the point of view of the people you serve and the people who pay for them is an absolute necessity if you are to become and remain a social entrepreneur.'

However, a social enterprise's self-assessment should go beyond simply updating its services. It must constantly review whether its fundamental goals and structures need to be revised, perhaps because of changing economic or political conditions or because the 'need' is now being met elsewhere. In CRAC's case, the process of re-evaluation led to the wholesale overhaul of the organisation in the mid-1970s. CRAC's Schools and Conferences Programmes were still a valuable resource for its client base but constricted its publishing activities. In an environment much changed from that into which CRAC emerged in 1964, the publishing division needed to expand in order to ensure it met market demand and could compete with commercial publishers, leading to CRAC giving birth to Hobsons and then to NICEC. The separation of interests and labours posed inherent risks to each of the constituent entities but the subsequent success of each confirmed that the decision was correct. Where CRAC may have become weighed down by its own structure, it was instead able to continue delivering effective and relevant services, partly through its own activities and partly through the new organisations it had germinated.

As this adjustment proved, the long-term success of a social enterprise is reliant on the ongoing assessment of day-to-day operations but also a willingness to undertake longer-term reviews that may result in difficult but necessary changes.

Meeting a Need, Not Building an Empire

The essential process of self-assessment in CRAC was made easier by the management team's ability to remain focused on its core aims and their delivery, as opposed to being caught up in personal ambition or growing the organisation for its own sake. Brickerhoff describes a good social entrepreneur in this way:

'*They always keep mission first, but know that without money, there is no mission output.*'

Bridgewater summed up CRAC's raison d'être as:

'*Meeting a need, not building an empire.*'

As Schumacher famously put it: '*Small is beautiful*'.

It was in this cause that the management team developed its system of nests (CRAC, Hobsons, NICEC, IMS [operating at a distance] and, later, ECCTIS), allowing each nest to find the space and ideal conditions to incubate its own 'eggs'. From its inception CRAC also worked with a wide array of partners, ranging from organisations including ACE, the Industrial Welfare Society and the Tavistock Institute, through to the Science Research Council, the Schools Council and relevant government departments. In addition, CRAC was in the business of disseminating best practice as it found it, whether through publications, conferences, courses or films. Those who benefited from these services could then spread the word further through their local networks. Thus CRAC was always willing to sow more seeds than it could develop itself. The decision to participate in projects was made on the basis of how best to make use of expertise and resources in pursuit of delivering CRAC's 'mission'. Sharing credit or, on occasion financial returns, was acceptable in the cause of meeting these wider aims.

A Blueprint for Social Enterprise
In the period of operation covered in the body of this book, CRAC provided a blueprint for modern social enterprises by having:
- a clear vision of what it wanted to achieve
- a cool-headed entrepreneurial approach which ensured that those projects that could make money did so, and those that were worthwhile but not self-sustaining could be funded (either from CRAC's own finances or external grants or sponsorship) and did not cripple the organisation
- an ability to recognise and develop innovative new means of meeting its aims
- a willingness to constantly appraise its activities and make difficult decisions in pursuit of its goals
- an understanding that it should be a catalyst for activities outside its own infrastructure.

Professor Tommy Wilson, who was involved with several major CRAC projects including the Headteachers as Managers courses and the Graduate Schools, strongly advised Bridgewater that CRAC should always see itself as a 'transitional institution', prepared to close down and move on if it had served its purpose. '*A social enterprise like CRAC must never forget that it exists to meet needs,*' he said.

As a social enterprise successfully fulfils its goals, it must evolve, either meeting new needs or accepting that its role is a transitional one. Should a social enterprise cease to innovate or move its focus from meeting needs to merely securing its own 'market position', its useful life may be considered over. Brickerhoff, once more, argues convincingly that constant progression is an inherent feature of the best and most successful social enterprises:

'*For the true social entrepreneur, there is always a next time, a next venture, a next service, a next product, a next alliance, a next project, a next person to serve.*'

Appendix A
CRAC Chronology: 1963-75

CRAC Landmarks	**National Developments**

1963

	Sir Alec Douglas-Home (Conservative) replaces Harold Macmillan (Conservative) as Prime Minister (October).
Bridgewater and Watts attend ACE Conference in Cambridge, distributing a pamphlet outlining ideas for a new organisation and also meeting Klaus Boehm.	Labour leader, Harold Wilson, gives his 'White Heat' speech on the technological revolution at his party conference.

The Newsom Report, *Half our Future,* looking at the education of 13-16 year olds of average and less than average ability, is published.

The Robbins Report on *Higher Education* is published, recommending a major expansion of the Higher Education sector. |

1964

| CRAC opens office at 25 St Andrews Street, Cambridge.

CRAC Survey of all UK secondary schools, which forms the basis of CRAC's first membership package.

CRAC's Council and Advisory Panel are established.

The first CRAC Membership promotion to schools offers a subscription to the *Journal*, several *Information Sheets* and two questions to the Question Service for a fee of 10 guineas.

First edition of the *Journal* includes much publicised article on manpower forecasting by Colin Leicester.

CRAC's first National Conference, on *Higher Education and Careers*, held at King's College, Cambridge.

FBI Grand Council gives CRAC the contract to run its *Careers Index Card* scheme. | Harold Wilson (Labour) replaces Douglas-Home as Prime Minister (October).

The Government's Manpower Research Unit makes its first report.

The Industrial Training Act comes into force, establishing an Industrial Training Board for each major industry. (CRAC consulted during its drafting.)

Heyworth Report on the *University Appointments Boards* published.

The Schools Council for the Curriculum and Examinations set up. |
|---|---|

CRAC Landmarks	National Developments

1965

Students in Transition - Survey and Information Bulletin published.

The first *Course Comparison Guides* are launched.

First 'Business Studies Courses for the Sixth-Form Leaver' held. 'Careers Library on a Shoestring' Programme begins.

Hooker Craigmyle & Co. appointed as fundraising consultants.

House of Commons hosts debate on careers guidance.

Lady Albemarle's Report, *The Future Development of the Youth Employment Service*, published.

Labour government publishes 'Circular 10/65', recommending the comprehensive schooling system.

1966

Creativity in School, a 30-minute documentary film produced by CRAC, premiers in Shell Centre London.

First 'Introduction into Business Methods' course for teachers run.

Which B.Ed, a guide to the new secondary teaching qualification, published.

CRAC creates a unique careers library classification scheme (CLIC), subsequently taken up by the Central Youth Employment Executive.

CRAC Scottish Office opens in Edinburgh.

First residential 'Undergraduate School' held at University College, Oxford.

First 'Challenge of Industry' course held, in conjunction with the Industrial Welfare Society.

Harold Wilson wins the general election.

The Occupational Guidance Service is established under the remit of the Department of Employment.

'Brain-drain' of UK scientists and engineers to USA attracts growing attention and concern.

1967

Conference for 'Executives Responsible for Interviewing Undergraduates' held at Church House, Westminster.

Middle School Choice, for pupils choosing O-levels, published.

'Turn or Return to Teaching' course begins.

CRAC and the Tavistock Institute runs a 'Secondary School Administration for the 1970s' course for headteachers.

1967 *continued*

First residential 'Graduate School' is held at University College, Oxford, run in conjunction with the Science Research Council.

The Standing Committee of University Appointments Services (SCUAS) is founded.

Connolly Occupational Interests Questionnaire launched, alongside related courses for careers teachers.

Tony Watts leaves for studies at York University.

CRAC staff write regular careers column for the *Financial Times*.

Adrian Bridgewater joins Ted Heath's pre-election advisory Education Policy Group.

1968

T.W. Harrington Jnr and M. Jacoby lead a CRAC seminar on 'American Recruitment Techniques '.

'Interview Techniques Training Programme Kit' launched.

The first *Perspective* film, about working in computers, is released with five further films following over the next three years.

The Swann Report, *The Flow into Employment of Scientists, Engineers and Technologists*, published.

CRAC moves offices to Bateman Street, Cambridge.

Institute of Manpower Studies established.

Upper School Choice, for pupils choosing their A-levels, published.

The Dainton Report, *The Flow of Candidates in Science and Technology to Higher Education*, published.

A Good Start in Life by Peter Daws published.

Beyond A Degree (later called *Graduate Employment and Training*) first published.

1969

Joint Careers Survey with NUT reveals 'worrying results'.

The Haslegrave Report, on *Technician Courses and Examinations*, published.

Further Education, edited by Willam van der Eyken, launched.

The Standing Conference of Employers of Graduates (SCOEG) is founded.

Rio Tinto Zinc provide CRAC with a loan of £25,000, repaid within two years.

The National Association of Careers Teachers (now the Association for Careers Education and Guidance) is founded.

CRAC Landmarks	National Developments

1970

Crowley Occupational Interests Blank launched.

Tony Watts returns to CRAC, having completed studies at York, to establish its Research and Development Unit.

CRAC runs its first 'Graduate School' in Scotland.

Ted Heath (Conservative) replaces Wilson as Prime Minister (June). Margaret Thatcher becomes Minister of State for Education and Science.

First National Careers Exhibition held at London Olympia.

1971

The Open University opens its doors to students.

The Times Higher Education Supplement is first published.

CRAC establishes a Business Studies Unit with sponsorship from Tube Investments.

1972

CRAC launches the *British Journal of Guidance and Counselling*.

The *Bull's Eye* series of illustrated children's booklets published.

1973

Decide for Yourself by Bill Law published.

CRAC buys the rights to *Graduate Studies*, a directory of postgraduate academic opportunities.

Adrian Bridgewater resigns as Director of CRAC to set up Hobsons, an independent publisher with an arms-length relationship with CRAC.

John Brodie takes over as CRAC Director.

The Employment and Training Act comes into force.

The Youth Employment Service is succeeded by the Careers Service.

1974

Rethink, a guide for sixth-formers needing to reconsider their post-school plans, published.

Hobsons begins publishing operations.

Harold Wilson (Labour) replaces Heath as Prime Minister (February).

The Manpower Services Commission is established.

1975

The National Institute for Careers Education and Counselling (NICEC) is established as a joint project of CRAC and Hatfield Polytechnic, with Tony Watts as Director.

Adrian Bridgewater joins the Open University Council.

Appendix B

Reprinted from the Director's last Report (1971–72)
before the separation of Hobsons, NICEC and CRAC

CRAC outlook and future plans
CRAC's objectives have remained unchanged since its inauguration in 1964. They are
* To act as a communication link between the worlds of education and of work, and
* To service and develop guidance work in schools, universities and colleges.

Although the objectives have remained constant over the past year, their method of execution has evolved and changed considerably, in part at least to meet the changing needs of guidance and careers work as it has developed in Britain.

At this stage in CRAC's history it is important to reflect on these changes in the field and to consider the part which , given adequate and suitable resources, CRAC could play in their further development.

Why guidance work is important
Careers guidance is concerned with the dynamic relationship between the individual and the society in which he lives. It is sometimes regarded by employers as a means of providing the recruits they want; those who actually work in the guidance field - by no means always excluding those working as personnel officers - tend by contrast to emphasise their responsibility to the individual. But either way, guidance has a crucial function to plan in helping individuals to find meaningful and satisfying roles in society and to produce a society which satisfies the needs of its members. There are other more specific reasons for the increasing recognition in Britain of the importance of guidance work:
* for Britain manpower is a major economic asset
* human wastage resulting from poor decision-making can be costly: it has been pointed out that if one adviser could present the wastage of only four 'student years' in higher education, each costing £800 to £1,200, he would be earning his keep.
* choices open to students are increasingly complex and varied
* society is increasingly concerned with equality of opportunity and with the need to broaden the occupational horizons and aspirations of students from socially-deprived backgrounds
* schools are increasingly concerned not just with what the student learns in cognitive terms, but with his personal development also
* more and more years are being spent in full-time education, which means that more of what Donald Super has termed the 'exploratory' stage of vocational development has to take place within the educational system
* educational choices have powerful vocational implications – indeed, education is more and more being asked to sort people into their places in society
* individuals are increasingly asserting their autonomy and their right to make the decisions that will determine their future rather than have these decisions imposed upon them; this means that selection processes must increasingly become the joint decisions of the selector and candidate.

The changing face of guidance work in Britain
The nine years' since CRAC was established in 1963/4 have seen an impressive range of developments including:

- *Almost all schools now have careers teachers, and in many cases they do more than merely handle information: they sometimes for instance have programmes of careers teaching within the curriculum. A National Association of Careers Teachers was founded in 1969. Training is still inadequate, but CRAC has helped to fill the gap through its programme of short courses*

- *A new brand of guidance worked has appeared in schools: the school counsellor. The first one-year full-time training courses were set up in 1965; there are now nine such courses, and several part-time courses as well. School counsellors cover educational and personal counselling as well as vocational guidance, and are trained not to offer advice but to help students to work through problems and reach decision with which they can identify. They have now formed a National Association of Educational Counsellors. CRAC has conducted research into the role of the counsellor and has published the only centralised information on relevant training courses.*

- *The 'youth employment officer' has become the 'careers officer', signifying an increasing concern with developmental guidance work rather than simply placement into jobs. The Institute of Careers Officers has played a major role in this change. CRAC has close links with the Central Youth Employment Executive, and has for instance developed with them a joint classification system for occupational information which is now used throughout the country.*

- *The concept of the 'careers team' has been extended beyond the professional groups directly responsible for guidance work to encompass all teachers. CRAC has run courses to develop the counselling skills of teachers in para-counselling roles (eg as house or form tutors), and to inform subject teachers about post-school opportunities related to their subjects.*

- *There has been a significant improvement in the quality of information on careers. To this CRAC has made a major contribution, particularly in two areas which were previously almost totally ignored: information on the range of oportunities in higher education and further education, and on the career implications of educational choices.*

- *A mass of materials have appeared for use in programmes of careers education within the curriculum – not just describing careers but also helping students to assess themselves and preparing them for the world of work. CRAC published the first major attemply to provide a basis for a course of this kind (Vocational Choice) and has since played a leading role both in publishing materials and in providing training on planning careers courses. It also helped to set up the Schools Council's curriculum development project on careers education and guidance. In many ways the emergence of 'careers education' has been the most significant development in careers work over the last eight years, for it has symbolised the fact that it is no longer a peripheral area but is now one of the school's central concerns.*

- *Increased use has been made of tests in guidance work. CRAC has published two interests questionnaires (Connolly and Crowley) and has run training courses in their use.*

- *There has been a significant growth of research and theoretical writing in the guidance field, helping to lay the foundations for better guidance practices. The chief centre for this work has been the Vocational Guidance Research Unit at the University of Leeds. CRAC publishes one of the unit's major monographs, A Good*

Start in Life, and is now launching the first British academic journal in the guidance field.

- *More concerted efforts have been made to involve parents in guidance work. CRAC has attempted to promote this through experiments involving careers shops in large stores and national careers exhibitions, and through makings its publications available both at parents' evenings and in bookshops.*
- *Counselling services have sprung up in further and higher education, and an Association for Student Counselling has been forned. Often these services exist alongside the existing appointments services, which at the university level have now set up a Standing Conference of University Appointments Services. CRAC publishes information to help the work of appointments officers, and has run undergraduate and graduate schools to introduce students to aspects of work in the public and private sectors.*
- *The government has set up 45 occupational guidance units to provide a free service for adults who are thinking of changing their career. There has also been a striking growth of independent vocational guidance agencies. CRAC has deliberately not provided a guidance service itself, but has circulated information on existing agencies to interested individuals.*
- *A Standing Conference for the Advancement of Counselling has been set up to co-ordinate the work of all the professional groups involved in counselling across a very broad front - ranging from medicine and law to education and social work - and the International Round Table for the Advancement of Counselling has provided a forum for international exchanges of information and opinion. CRAC is represented on the Executive Committees of both these bodies.*

From these developments five major trends can be identified:

- *An increasing emphasis on giving students information and teaching them how to handle it rather than recommending a particular career.*
- *An increasing emphasis on a developmental approach to guidance, preparing students for choices over a long period of time, rather than a crisis-oriented approach.*
- *An increasing recognition of the relevance of guidance work to the school curriculum as a whole.*
- *An increasing emphasis on the inter-relationship of educational, vocational and personal decisions.*
- *An increasing professionalisation of guidance services, side-by-side with an increasing attempt to harness and service the other likely sources of influence on students' choices.*

The future of guidance work

It seems likely that all the trends we have identified will continue over the next five years. At the same time, there are at least four additional forces which are likely influence the future development of guidance services:

- *More individualised learning and course-planning in schools. Students will be given increasing choice not only in the subjects they study but also in curriculum content, teaching resources, examination methods, etc. This is implicit in the emphasis on learning rather than teaching which is likely to accelerate over the next few years.*
- *The present high level of unemployment may not be just a passing phase but may*

be the first concrete sign that post-industrial society is likely to require fewer and fewer man-hours to be employed in 'productive' work.
- *The pace of occupational change means that new career choices will probably have to be made at several stages through an individual's life.*
- *With the Common Market mobility in terms of both higher education and jobs will increase in Europe.*

The responses of guidance to these forces are likely to include:
- *More world-oriented guidance and information services.*
- *Less work-oriented guidance services. Guidance work will become increasingly concerned with helping individuals to determine their whole life-style - including leisure, family and community roles - instead of concentrating so heavily as at present on choice of occupation.*
- *Development of adult guidance services to help people with the career and life-style decisions which they will increasingly have to take throughout their lives.*
- *Increasing emphasis at school level on teaching decision-making skills.*
- *Increasing use of technology - notably computers and audio-visual information systems - to cope with the growing pressures on guidance work and to allow guidance workers to concentrate more on the counselling work which they alone can do.*

The future role of CRAC
As has been seen, CRAC has played a significant role in the development of guidance services over the last few years. The part that it can play in the future will largely depend on the extent to which it can develop and change its own organisational and financial structure to grapple with a national, if not worldwide, set of needs.

The three areas in which it would hope to provide services are:

*1 **Publications and services for guidance work** - not only for secondary schools but also for guidance work in further and higher education and with adults.*

CRAC's existing range of publications will be maintained and updated regularly, but possible development areas include:

(a) Largely unexplored areas of information on occupations.
- *Psycho-social aspects of jobs (implications for life-style etc.)*
- *Forecasts of future supply and demand by occupations*
- *Transferability between occupations*
- *Opportunities within the Common Market.*
(b) Largely unexplored areas of information on further and higher education:
- *Psycho-social aspects (the 'atmosphere' of colleges, etc.)*
- *Comparative information on sub-degree-level courses (HND, the new Diploma in Higher Education, etc.)*
- *Educational opportunities within the Common Market, and transferability of qualifications between countries.*
(c) Classroom materials for simulating particular occupations.
(d) Classroom materials for teaching decision-making skills.
(e) Careers education materials for primary and middle schools.
(f) Classroom materials in the wide areas of leisure and of moral and social education.

In addition, CRAC plans to develop the application of new media both to its existing areas of interest and to the development areas:
(i)   Audiovisual media
(ii) Gaming and simulation techniques
(iii) Computers

2   **Courses.** *Almost all CRAC courses are heavily oversubscribed, and demand clearly exceeds supply. CRAC will continue to run a major school course programme, though it may run some courses for guidance workers outisde secondary schools, and its teachers' courses will probably become more specialised as more basic training courses become available. In adddition, CRAC hopes to suppport the expansion of basic training, much of which will be done on a localised basis, by establishing a courses resource centre on which course organisers can draw. This should include the development of modules in areas where CRAC has particular expertise, for use in courses being run elsewhere, and also supporting materials – tapes, slides, papers, etc.*

3   **Research work.** *CRAC is exploring the possibility of establishing a Research Unit at a university or polytechnic, which will undertake fundamental research. CRAC plans to allocate some of its resources to this unit, and to ensure close contacts by establishing at least one joint appointment. Because many people consider expenditure on research either as a meaningless search for status or merely as a necessary evil, some areas in which research could immediately help in the development of guidance services are outlined below. They represent no more than starting points for discussion and, taken together, are clearly well beyond the reach of CRAC's existing resources.*

A   ***Measurement of effectiveness of guidance techniques and materials***.

Two different types are required:
(a) Development of measuring instruments, eg
*   •   criteria of occupational success;*
*   •   inventory of vocational maturity.*

(b) Application of these (and other) instruments to measure effectiveness of e.g.
*   •   guidance work in general (effects on truancy rates, motivating pupils to find school meaningful, etc);*
*   •   different counselling styles and techniques;*
*   •   ways of teaching decision-making skills;*
*   •   ways of promoting personal growth and maturation;*
*   •   ways of helping people to cope with change and transition;*
*   •   different media for conveying psycho-social information about work;*
*   •   specific careers education materials, e.g. CRAC publications.*

B   **Career pattern studies**
(a) Testing developmental theories of occupational choice in Britain, including enquiries into students' cognitive maps, the way they acquire occupational information, etc.

(b)   Studies of career development and career mobility. One of the main objects of such studies would be to distinguish between different types of job changing, and to develop both concepts and information which could infuse guidance work.

(c)   Follow-up of entrants to particular courses or occupations, partly to provide data to be fed back to potential subsequent entrants, e.g.

•   sixth-form modern linguists;

•   entrants to teaching profession.

(d)   Studies of the relationship between work and leisure, and between occupational roles and non-occupational roles, e.g.

•   effect of subcultural identity on occupational choice (e.g. at university).

C   Higher education studies:

(a)   Studies of university and college environments, partly to provide data to be fed back to prospective students.

(b)   Studies of the effects of an interim between school and higher education on degree performances, satisfaction with course choices, and vocational maturity.

D   Descriptive studies of guidance work:

(a)   Describing ways in which the main objectives of careers education are met, or not met, in a sample of schools.

(b)   Describing how careers officers use occupational information in the guidance situation.

(c)   Conducting a task-analysis of the careers teacher's role in a sample of schools.

(d)   Itemising the opportunities for decision-making provided in a sample of school environments.

General summary

Reporting on 1970/71 I commented that that year might prove a water-shed for CRAC and for guidance as a whole.

Developments of the past year have confirmed the accuracy of that commentary. With the rapid growth in the recognition of the need for the range of services which CRAC can provide, the key issue now confronting CRAC is to find the right financial and organisational structure. It is vital that CRAC should be able to respond to the demands which will be placed upon it. And as guidance becomes increasingly recognised as a central concern of all educational institutions, so CRAC should be capable of servicing needs and developing an understanding of the changing needs of guidance.

Cambridge, October 1972

Appendix C
Reference Sources

Introduction

Brinckerhoff, Peter C. (2000), *Social Entrepreneurship: The Art of Mission-Based Venture Development.* Wiley.

Chapter One

Association of Teachers in Technical Institutions (1964), *Is Robbins Enough?: A commentary on the Robbins report.*

Carr Report (1958), *Training for Skill: Recruitment and Training of Young Workers in Industry.* HMSO.

Carter, M. (1962), *Home, School and Work: A Study of the Education and Employment of Young People in Britain.* Pergamon Press.

Crowther Report (1959), *Report of the Central Advisory Council for Education (England).* HMSO.

Hines, B. (1968), *A Kestrel for a Knave.* Michael Joseph.

Law, B. & Watts, A. G. (1977), *Schools, Careers and Community.* CIO Publishing.

Ministry of Education (1947), *The New Secondary Education,* Pamphlet No. 9. HMSO.

Norwood Report (1943), *Report of the Committee of the Secondary Schools Examination Council on Curriculum and Examinations in Secondary Schools.* HMSO.

Sampson, A. (1971), *The New Anatomy of Britain.* Hodder & Stoughton.

White Paper (1943), *Educational Reconstruction.* HMSO.

White Paper (1956), *Technical Education.* HMSO.

Wilson, H., Speech to the Labour Party Conference, 1 October 1963.

Chapter Two

ACE (1960), *Where (Vol. 1).* The Advisory Centre for Education.

Acton Society Trust (1956), *Management Succession: The Recruitment, Selection, Training and Promotion of Management.* Acton Society Trust.

Albemarle Report (1965), *The Future Development of the Youth Employment Service.* HMSO.

Carter, M. (1966), *Into Work.* Penguin.

Crowther Report (1959), *Report of the Central Advisory Council for Education (England).* HMSO.

APPENDIX C

Dryden, W. & Watts, A. G. (1993), *Guidance & Counselling in Britain: A 20-year Perspective*. Hobsons Publishing.

Federation of British Industries (1965), *University Appointments Boards: Comment by the Federation of British Industries on the Heyworth Report*. Federation of British Industries.

Heyworth Report (1964), *University Appointments Boards*. HMSO.

Ince, G. H., Sir, (1949), *The Development of the Youth Employment Service*. (Margate Conference, Easter, 1949). National Union of Teachers.

www.makingthemodernworld.org.uk.

Newsom Report (1963), *Half our Future*. HMSO.

Peck, D. (2004), *Careers Services: History, Policy and Practice in the United Kingdom*. RoutledgeFalmer.

Powell, E. (1968), Speech at Bowness, Windermere, 17 February.

Rogers, P. (1993), 'The Graduate Recruitment Scene Pre-1962'. *Graduate Recruitment: A 25-year Retrospective*. Hobsons Publishing.

Sampson, A. (1962), *The Anatomy of Britain*. Hodder & Stoughton.

Sampson, A. (1965), *The New Anatomy of Britain*. Hodder & Stoughton.

Whitehead, A. N. (1929), *The Aims of Education*. Williams and Norgate Limited.

Young, M. (1958), *The Rise of the Meritocracy*. Penguin.

Chapter Three

Author's interview with Deborah Bevan, 20 May 2009.

Author's interview with Mary Munro, 4 June 2009.

Robins Report (1963), *Report of the Committee on Higher Education*. HMSO.

The Report of the Director (1966). CRAC.

Tomlinson, J. C., 'A Central Careers Library' in *Library Association Record,* 2 February 1967.

Chapter Four

Author's interview with Brian MacArthur, 22 May 2009.

'Careers Advice' in *Personnel Management Journal,* December 1964.

http://hansard.millbanksystems.com/commons/1965/feb/05/youth-employment-service.

Leicester, C., 'Economic Growth and the School Leaver' in *CRAC Journal,* Summer 1964.

Statement of Principal Activities, CRAC, 1967.

The Report of the Director, CRAC, 1966.

Tomlinson, J. C., 'A Central Careers Library' in *Library Association Record*, 2 February 1967.

Watts, A. G., Letter in *New Society,* 10 December 1964.

Chapter Five

Annual Report, CRAC, 1970.

Annual Report, CRAC, 1973.

Astryx, 'Room at the Top' in *The Times Educational Supplement,* 22 March 1968.

Author's interview with David Blandford, 5 May 2009.

Author's interview with Mike Leonard, 4 June 2009.

'Catching the Audience's Eye' in *The Financial Times*, 14 January 1969.

Classified advert, CRAC, 1967.

'CRAC Down on Computers' in *Teacher,* 3 November 1967.

'Finding Tomorrow's Managers' in *Management Today*, December 1966.

'Integrating the PhDs' in *The Times,* 14 September 1967.

'Making Better Careers Decisions' in *The Times Review of Industry*, November 1966.

'Of Low Degree' in *The Spectator*, 29 July 1966.

'Progressives' in *Technical Education,* 5 May 1969.

Statement of Principal Activities, CRAC, 1967.

'Swann Song at Oxford' in *The New Scientist,* 21 September 1967.

The Report of the Director, CRAC, 1966.

'University to Industry' in *Journal of Fisons,* December 1966.

Chapter Six

Author's interview with Geoff Cooksey, 27 May 2009.

Callaghan, J., Speech at Ruskin College, Oxford, 18 October 1976.

Cherry, N. (1974), 'Do Careers Officers Give Good Advice?' in *British Journal of Guidance and Counselling,* 1974.

Dainton Report (1968), *Enquiry into the Flow of Candidates in Science and Technology into Higher Education*. HMSO.

Department of Education and Science (1973), *Employment and Training Act*. HMSO.

Hawthorn, R. Kidd, J. M., Killeen, J., Law, B. & Watts, A. G. (Eds) (1996), *Rethinking Careers Education and Guidance: Theory, Policy and Practice*. Routledge.

Heyworth Report (1964), *University Appointments Boards*. HMSO.

Kirkman, W. (2007), 'SCUAS: Conception, Birth and Early Growth' in *Reflections on Change, 1967-2007* (Eds, Butler, T. & Dane, M.). SCUAS.

Peck, D. (2004), *Careers Services: History, Policy and Practice in the United Kingdom.* RoutledgeFalmer.

Robins Report (1963)*, Report of the Committee on Higher Education.* HMSO.

Smith, A. R. & Bartholomew, D. J., 'Manpower Planning in the United Kingdom: An Historical Review' in *The Journal of the Operational Research Society.* March 1988.

Chapter Seven

Director's Interim Report, CRAC, 1979.

Hans Hoxter Obituary, *The Guardian,* 29 November 2002.

Chapter Eight

Annual Report, Hobsons Publishing, 1987.

Author's interview with John Brodie, 18 May 2009.

http://www.prospects.ac.uk/nicec/distance-learning-unit/DLUnit2/DOTS.html.

Chapter Nine

Author's interview with Alan Jamieson, 18 May 2009.

Brinckerhoff, Peter C. (2000), *Social Entrepreneurship: The Art of Mission-Based Venture Development.* Wiley.

Paton, Rob (2002), *Managing and Measuring Social Enterprise*. Sage.

Spreckley, Freer (1981), *Social Audit – A Management Tool for Co-operative Working.* Beechwood College, Leeds.

About the author

Daniel Smith is a freelance author and editor, which suggests that he never took any notice of his own careers advisor. He studied English and History at Cardiff University before working on *The Statesman's Yearbook,* the renowned geo-political guide to the world. His subsequent career has included a stint with Seagull Books, the publishing arm of a not-for-profit social arts organisation in Kolkata, India.

His books include *World in Your Pocket, The Sherlock Holmes Companion: An Elementary Guide, The Lucky Bugger's Casebook: Tales of Serendipity and Outrageous Good Fortune* and *Forgotten Firsts: A Compendium of Lost Pioneers, Trend-Setters and Guinea Pigs*. He lives in East London with Rosie.